D0426456

CRITICAL ANTHOLOGIES OF NONFICTION WRITING™

CRITICAL PERSPECTIVES ON 9/11

Edited by
FLETCHER HAULLEY

THE ROSEN PUBLISHING GROUP, INC.
NEW YORK

Published in 2005 by The Rosen Publishing Group, Inc.
29 East 21st Street, New York, NY 10010

Copyright © 2005 by The Rosen Publishing Group, Inc.

All rights reserved. No part of this book may be reproduced in any
form without permission in writing from the publisher, except by a
reviewer.

First Edition

Library of Congress Cataloging-in-Publication Data

Critical perspectives on 9/11 / edited by Fletcher Haulley.—1st ed.
    p. cm.— (Critical anthologies of nonfiction writing)
Includes bibliographical references and index.
Contents: Time, continuity, and change: terrorism arrives on American
shores—People, places, and environments : community in the wake of
September 11—Individual development and identity : the birth of a
terrorist and the deaths of heroes—Science, technology, and society :
understanding a new kind of warfare—Global connections: the
United States and the world beyond its shores.
ISBN 1-4042-0060-6 (library binding)
1. September 11 Terrorist Attacks, 2001—Juvenile literature. 2. War
on Terrorism, 2001—Juvenile literature. [1. September 11 Terrorist
Attacks, 2001—Sources. 2. War on Terrorism, 2001—Sources.]
I. Title: Critical perspectives on 911. II. Haulley, Fletcher.
III. Series.

HV6432.7.C75 2005
973.931—dc22
                                                    2003027572

Manufactured in the United States of America

On the cover: Firemen and rescue workers comb through the
wreckage of the World Trade Center soon after the terrorist
attacks of September 11, 2001, searching for survivors and
victims' remains.

CONTENTS

LIBRARY
DEXTER SCHOOLS
DEXTER, NM 88230

INTRODUCTION

he terrorist attacks of September 11, 2001—in which four commercial jets were hijacked and flown into the Pentagon outside Washington, D.C., the World Trade Center in New York City, and a Pennsylvania field—were events so enormous in their intensity and significance that everyone who lived through that day will remember exactly where they were when planes began falling from the sky and mighty buildings crumbled. It was easy enough to hope and believe that the first plane's crash into the north tower of the World Trade Center was a terrible accident. The instant the second plane crashed into the south tower at 9:03 AM, however, everyone watching from the streets and across the nation came to the sickening realization that what they were seeing was no accident. It was a deliberate terrorist attack against the United States.

Within minutes, a third plane had crashed into the Pentagon—the very heart of America's military defense—and reports of a fourth plane downed during a struggle between passengers and the terrorists began to trickle in. This cascade of attacks was all the more shocking because the United States had, for so much of its history, seemed invulnerable to attacks on its soil. After all, it is naturally protected and buffered by two wide oceans and is sandwiched between two friendly and allied nations—Canada and Mexico. Terrorism against American citizens and the government had occurred mostly overseas and did not seem to pose a real threat to average Americans. The few terrorist attacks that had occurred on American soil—such as Timothy McVeigh's bombing of the Murrah Federal Building in Oklahoma City or "Unabomber" Ted Kaczynski's mail bombs sent to prominent scientists and executives—could not shake Americans' sense of security. Sure, the occasional homegrown fanatic would blow something up to make a political point, but it always seemed to happen elsewhere, to other people.

The terror and devastation of the September 11 attacks destroyed Americans' sense of security. The long lists of the dead and missing and the visible carnage in the wreckage of the towers made it clear to all Americans that they were no longer safe from militant groups around the world who have grievances against the United States. Now, many citizens fear for the safety of every landmark across the country. Now, many are concerned about the vulnerability of every power plant, especially the nuclear generators. Now, many worry about the tempting target posed by large gatherings of crowds, in shopping malls or sports stadiums, for example. Now, the United States government regularly provides color-coded terrorist threat warnings to police departments and ordinary citizens alike, asking vigilance of both.

September 11, 2001, shattered Americans' perceptions of the world and their homeland, and security concerns and procedures that once would have seemed unthinkable are now part of everyday life.

On that terrible day, many innocent people died. Among the long list of the missing were the names of hundreds of police officers, firefighters, and other emergency workers.

These men and women died trying to save others' lives. When many were running away from the burning buildings, these men and women were running into them. The courage and compassion that this must have required are immense and unfathomable. If a comforting silver lining can be found in this story, it may be the heroism of these rescue workers. Their acts of selflessness were so grand and heroic that they have entered the realm of popular folklore, and for good reason. While the attacks have left America fearful, they have also shown that basic human goodness and caring exist in average people, even in times of extreme fear, hatred, and violence.

This anthology movingly bears witness to the day's heroes. It also seeks to gain insight into the terrorists who sent almost 3,000 innocent people to their deaths. The September 11 attacks were perpetrated by murderous fanatics. Specifically, the killers were Islamic fundamentalist terrorists. These militants consider everyone who does not follow their strict interpretation of the Koran—the Muslim holy book written more than 1,300 years ago—as the enemy. They feel the Koran instructs them to kill the enemy in God's name. While these people's actions can never be justified, there is a reason that their groups exist and their angry and hate-filled message continues to gain enthusiastic support in certain areas around the world.

Many nations of the Middle East—the breeding ground for much Islamic terrorist activity—are controlled by non-democratic governments that tell their people what to believe and how to act. When they disobey, they are violently punished. The United States has often supported these repressive governments for a variety of strategic and economic reasons. When the people of these countries see that they have no basic rights and are often desperately poor while their leaders live like kings, they look for someone to blame. The United States often becomes a convenient target. After the September 11 attacks, many questions were raised about the United States' role in the world and how that role might have led to or invited these attacks. The American and British occupation of Iraq, following the 2003 invasion of the country, has forced this question back into the public consciousness. Many wonder if an aggressive foreign policy, backed by the threat of military attack, is exactly the sort of global bullying that makes members of other nations hate America and wish to see it destroyed. These agonized, angry, soul-searching questions are examined in this anthology, though clear-cut answers remain hard to come by.

By the second anniversary of the September 11 attacks, much had changed in New York, Washington, and throughout the country. The sense of urgency and compassion so strongly felt in the days and months after the attacks had dissipated. Gone, too, was the sense of disbelief, the feeling that these events could not possibly have happened, that it was all just a terrible dream. This anthology seeks to re-create the surreal mood of the days and months that immediately followed the September 11 attacks, the overwhelming shock and grief coupled with an urgent search for understanding. As journalists covered the event and its fallout, their writing contained an electricity in every letter typed. They wrote without certainty, trying instead to find where a single piece of information or insight could fit into this new and complex puzzle.

Each essay and article written during this time attempted to add a small bit of understanding to these events that were nearly impossible to understand.

In choosing and compiling this anthology's selections, primary sources drawn from September 11's immediate aftermath have purposely been favored over selections written with the benefit of hindsight or greater critical distance. This anthology is intended to be a slice of history as it unfolded. Not only should the important events of the day and its aftermath be understood, but the emotions of the time should be recovered as well. In many of the selections, the authors' words clearly betray their own emotions and perspectives. In revisiting a historical event that shook us to the core, the arrangement of these selections attempts to re-create the chaos and the first dawning of understanding of this boundless tragedy.

CHAPTER ONE

TIME, CONTINUITY, AND CHANGE: TERRORISM ARRIVES ON AMERICAN SHORES

Two Seconds Under the World: Terror Comes to America—The Conspiracy Behind the World Trade Center Bombing

By Jim Dwyer, David Kocieniewski,
Deidre Murphy, and Peg Tyre
1994

Al Qaeda terrorists destroyed the World Trade Center in New York City on September 11, 2001, but this was not the first time the towers had been the target of the group. On February 26, 1993, Al Qaeda terrorists parked a rented moving van filled with explosives in the center's underground garage. They planned to topple the south tower onto the nearby north tower, bringing both down in what would have been a far more destructive and deadly attack than even that seen on September 11. In the end, the explosion proved to be too weak to topple the towers or even cause serious damage to the buildings' structure, but the terrorists' message had been clear—the war of the Islamic fundamentalists had reached America's shores. Al Qaeda had signaled that from this

*point on, violence against American targets would follow
no conventional and accepted rules of warfare. Average citizens, including women and children, would now be targeted.
The call of jihad—the Muslim struggle against "infidels," or
nonbelievers—would provide all the justification necessary
for the murder of innocents.* New York Newsday *reporters
Jim Dwyer, David Kocieniewski, Deidre Murphy, and Peg
Tyre shared a Pulitzer Prize for their reporting on this event.*

---□---

The Parking Ramp
B-2 Level
World Trade Center
12:17:36 P.M.

The Ford Econoline van, built by the hundreds of thousands,
is the most popular commercial van in the country, next to
the Dodge Ram. They are bought by the thousands by small
businesses and government agencies. The Port Authority of
New York and New Jersey owns hundreds of Dodge Rams.
The Ryder Truck and Van Rental Company buys thousands
of its cousin, the Ford Econoline, every year for its short-
haul customers.

The Ford Econoline parked on the ramp of the B-2 level
today was owned by Ryder. It had been rented three days earlier at a Ryder outpost across the Hudson River in Jersey City,
not four miles from the Trade Center.

This van was not the largest of the Econolines sold by
Ford, but it could carry about 2,000 pounds of cargo, which
was plenty for this job. All of Ryder's trucks are painted yellow,

just like the Port Authority's. This one was built at a Ford plant in 1990. It had 295 cubic yards of cargo space. A long, cushioned bench extended from the driver's window to the passenger side. This was the only seating in the van.

Behind the driver's seat was a metal grid that separated the cargo from the passenger and driver, to prevent the stuff in the back from sliding forward and hitting anyone seated in the front. That was a particularly useful feature, considering the cargo. It consisted of 1,500 pounds of explosives, mixed in a vat in a storage locker in Jersey City. The explosives were connected to four twenty-foot fuses threaded through surgical tubing. The tubing suppressed smoke and slowed the rate of burn, extending it from ten minutes to maybe twenty. The bulk of the bomb was a gooey paste that lay in four cardboard boxes. Stacked alongside the boxes were three red metal cylinders of compressed hydrogen, each four feet long. In addition, four containers of nitroglycerin were loaded next to the goo in the boxes. A blasting packet of gunpowder was attached to each of the nitroglycerin containers. The fuses in the surgical tubing ran into the gunpowder, which would ignite the nitro. This, in turn, would detonate both the hydrogen gas and the gooey paste, which consisted primarily of urea, nitric acid, old newspapers, and paper bags.

The fuses had been burning for about fifteen minutes, or ever since the purchasing agent had pulled the yellow Port Authority van out of this parking space on a ramp that led from the garage. The Ryder van had then pulled in and taken the same space. It was not a legal spot, but the rented yellow van had the look and color of a Port Authority vehicle, and it wouldn't matter for very long, anyway. The two men in the Ryder van had flicked a cheap lighter and laid the flame against the fuses. Then they had stepped into a red car that had trailed them. Since they had not used a legal parking space, they had not passed through any of the toll gates, and they were able to loop out of the area without paying. The fuses they left behind smoldered. Thanks to the surgical tubing, the smoke was minimal. No one saw anything. . .

B-2 Level
World Trade Center
12:17:37 P.M.

The flames raced across the four fuses, an inch every two and a half seconds. Each fuse fed into a different blasting cap. All four fuses had the same rating: ten-minute fuses, twenty feet long. But one fuse would burn to zero inches first and touch off its blasting cap before anything else. Then all the other fuses would become immaterial, because the laws of thermodynamics would take over. Explosives are called energetic materials, because they release great bursts of energy when a solid or liquid is converted to a gas. When the first spark from the first fuse licked into the gunpowder, it would ignite the total explosion.

The gunpowder was packed in Atlas Rockmaster blasting caps, devices used probably hundreds of times a day in the United States to excavate building sites and in mining. The purpose of such a cap is to increase the pressure on the minute flakes that make up gunpowder. The same quantity of gunpowder, sprinkled in a line along the ground, would ignite and burn at a relatively slow rate, but it would not explode. It is the pressure of being confined in a cap that accelerates the rate of burn. The ignition of the powder began and finished within a single millisecond. At the instant when the powder was fully consumed, the pressure inside the cap rose to one thousand atmospheres, about 15,000 pounds per square inch. The gunpowder turned into a gas, carbon dioxide, and water, in the form of a high pressure vapor. The gas demanded more space than the powder did, and it expanded rapidly, bursting open the container of the cap. With that explosion—probably not audible more than a few yards away from the truck—the starting impulse of the entire 1,500-pound bomb had been generated, in the form of a concussion wave. The wave smacked into the first container of nitroglycerin, a liquid compound that decomposes and explodes upon impact.

The detonation of the nitroglycerin—that is, the speed at which the reaction moved through the bottle—was about 275,000 feet per second. In the time a person needs to read and recognize the word time, the nitroglycerin no longer existed. It had chemically changed into gas under immense pressure—about ten thousand atmospheres, or 150,000 pounds per square inch—and heat, in the area of 1,250 degrees centigrade. From the detonation triggered by the first bottle came an enormous concussion that detonated the unexploded nitroglycerin in the other three bottles in the truck. Three of the four fuses could have failed, and the bomb would have gone off.

The final phase of the explosion took place in the cardboard boxes. All explosions consist of fuel and a source of oxygen, known as the oxidizer. Here the urea pellets were the fuel; the oxidizer was the sulfuric acid. The mixture was not considered a "sensitive explosive," so the bomb makers devised the nitroglycerin cocktail to get them started. The ball of high-pressure gas from the nitroglycerin expanded, and its great pressure brought into reaction the sulfuric acid and the urea pellets. With a terrible, crawling rumble, like the roll of thunder across an August sky, the whole mass was transformed from a sodden paste into hot gas. Each kilogram of explosive created ten cubic yards of hot gas. The gas devoured the cardboard boxes that had contained the paste and moved outward until it hit the metal walls of the truck. Everything was moving under pressures of thousands of atmospheres. The walls of the van were torn into pieces moving faster than bullets. The concussion wave of expanding gas created a tornado-level wind, ripping through the underground garage. It hit the wall of the tower with a force of 1,500 pounds of pressure per square centimeter. This turned the cinder block wall into dust, and ripped a steel diagonal beam, weighing 14,000 pounds from its welds. Masonry walls collapsed.

Technically, the bomb had failed in its goal, which was to topple the 107-story building into its twin a few yards away. After the initial explosion of nitroglycerin and the paste in the boxes, the apparent intention of the bombers was that a secondary explosion would be fired from the hydrogen tanks. (Liquid hydrogen is used as rocket fuel.) The theory behind two, phased explosions was to first stretch the structure of the building—the atomic bonds of the steel columns and structural members. Then, they would be hit with a second blast while they were still distorted from the first explosion, and before they had contracted to their normal shape, hit them with a second explosion. But the timing was difficult to calibrate, and explosions of the tanks in the Ryder truck, near the end of the detonation of the urea bomb, served only to intensify the heat and pressure.

Because the truck had been parked at the base of the north tower, the effect of the explosion was roughly doubled. Just as the containment of the blasting cap increased the power of the initial explosion, the structural steel along the bottom of the tower also increased the pressure. While all the concrete walls collapsed, the vertical steel did not flinch. The bulk of the explosion was reflected away from the tower building. In effect, 1 World Trade Center had been turned into the world's largest blasting cap. A "mirror" effect was created by the strength of the tower base, roughly doubling the explosive forces and deflecting them into the garage.

The van had been sitting on an eleven-inch concrete slab, reinforced by steel. The concrete disintegrated into tiny rocks. The explosion went upward, blowing through another eleven inches of concrete overhead, then up another story, through another concrete roof, where it picked up a woman sitting at an airline ticket counter three stories above, and flung her thirty feet. Inside the garage, the gas concussion tore through cars and cinder blocks and found a ramp that allowed it to vent. A man waiting in a car at a light on West Street, three hundred feet from ground zero, felt a wind roar through his car. That made no sense, because all the windows were rolled up. He turned around and found his rear windshield blown open. Much of the floor of the B-2 level collapsed.

Wilfredo Mercado, the receiving agent for Windows on the World who was napping one floor above, was ejected from the room and landed headfirst five floors down, still seated in his chair. He was buried under twelve feet of concrete.

Room 107
B-2 Level
World Trade Center
12:17:37 P.M.

The explosion seared the pattern lines of Monica Smith's green sweater into her shoulder and back. All time values now vanish. Yet an instant unfolded and swallowed six lives, aged thirty-five and sixty-one and fifty-eight and thirty-seven and forty-five and forty-seven: 282 years of living. The greatest force of the explosion had been deflected away from the base of the tower, where the Port Authority workers were having their lunch. Yet there was more than enough to kill. Monica, seven months pregnant, was hit with the concussive blast and cement blocks. She suffered immediate "acoustic injuries" that killed her instantly by tearing apart her lungs and arteries. The blocks crashed across her head, ripping at her scalp. Had she not already died from the hurricane of air, the rubble would have finished her. Her shoulders and ribs were broken. Her other internal organs were torn. Her pelvis was fractured and her leg was broken. Her seven-month-old male fetus died from injuries that were very similar to his mother's. The Smiths had planned to call him Eddie.

The blast continued across the hall, into the next room, Steve Knapp's lunchroom. Nearest the wall and the bomb was Bob Kirkpatrick, the chief locksmith and genius handyman. He was leaning against the wall, having finished his lunch, a man six months away from retirement. His skull was fractured by a tremendous blow from a pipe that had been propelled from a ceiling over his head faster than any bullet. The great mechanical mind was dead. The left side of his chest was flattened when he was hurled against cinder blocks, then crushed by them.

Bill Macko was seated next to Kirkpatrick. When he'd left home that morning, he'd stopped at a candy store in Bayonne to buy a lottery ticket. "Give me a winner," Macko had said. "I don't want to work anymore." Funny, Wilfredo Mercado, almost directly over his head, had bought a lottery ticket, too. The explosion fired concrete pellets into the left side of his face. His left shoulder was separated and all his vertebrae were broken. His spleen and kidney were torn; so were the arteries that fed them. These, too, were acoustic injuries, the gases filling his body so quickly that no blood vessel or lung could survive the pressure. His intestines were ripped from the wall of his abdomen. Like everyone else caught in the blast, he appeared to have fallen from a twenty-story building.

Stephen Knapp, Vietnam veteran, who fished at sunset in the Great Kill waters, who brought eggplant parmigiana from home to his pregnant friend Monica Smith, and who took the great love of his life on their first date to Liberty Bell racetrack, probably was the last person in the room to die.

Monica had been the first. The blast killed serially: Smith, then Kirkpatrick, then Macko, then Knapp. It started by imprinting Monica Smith's green sweater onto her skin. It finished by firing particles of concrete into the white of Steve Knapp's left eye at a thousand miles per second. The fastest reflex in the human body shuts the eyelid. But Knapp's eyes did not close. From Monica Smith to Steve Knapp, death ran faster than the blink of an eye.

Al-Qaeda: In Search of the Terror Network That Threatens the World
By Jane Corbin
2003

The events of September 11, 2001, are now seared in every American's mind. Yet at the time of the first hijacked plane's crash into the north tower of the World Trade Center, nothing was known for sure about what was unfolding. Most news media were reporting that a plane had crashed into the World Trade Center, most likely due to an accident of some sort. Every news outlet dutifully reported on how, a half-century earlier, a B-25 had crashed into the Empire State Building after losing its bearings in a heavy fog. Surely, something similar had happened once again. However, within seventeen minutes, all Americans realized that this was no accident. With the second plane's crash into the south tower, the hopeful possibility that this was just a tragic accident evaporated. Without a doubt, terrorists were unleashing one of the very worst attacks on American soil ever. What follows is a detailed account of the day's events. While vividly describing the attacks, award-winning senior British Broadcasting Corporation correspondent Jane Corbin also relates the activities and reactions of many of the American government's most important figures on one of the darkest days in American history.

———□———

September 11

"Oh my God, the crew has been killed, a flight attendant has been stabbed—we've been hijacked!"
—Flight attendant aboard United Airlines Flight 175

The morning of 11 September 2001 was clear and sunny with a hint of the autumn to come in the woods around Boston when, at 8:00 A.M., American Airlines Flight 11 pushed back from Gate 26 at Logan airport. The captain, 52-year-old John Ogonowski, and his ten crew members anticipated a quiet run to Los Angeles with only eighty-one passengers aboard the Boeing 767. After take-off, at 8:13 A.M., the pilot received instructions from the control tower to turn twenty degrees to the right. "Twenty right AA-11," responded Ogonowski. He was then told to climb to 35,000 feet, the plane's cruising altitude. There was no response to this instruction.

The next transmission came ten minutes later, not from the captain but from a man speaking in heavily accented English: "We have some planes, just stay quiet and you will be okay," said the voice. The speaker thought he had only keyed the plane's public-address system, but one of the two pilots had surreptitiously pressed the microphone button on the plane's control stick, so controllers on the ground could hear the announcement. A whispered mobile-phone call was received by a ground worker from Madeline Sweeney, a flight attendant, to say that four hijackers were aboard the plane. "A hijacker cut the throat of a business-class passenger and he appears to be dead," she relayed back. Four hijackers had stormed the front of the plane and "had just gained access to the cockpit." Sweeney tried to call the cockpit but got no response.

Almost immediately the plane changed direction, turning south towards New York City, and began to descend. The transponder stopped transmitting its signal indicating the plane's flight number and altitude. Someone on board must have known to switch it off, making it harder to track the plane's progress. Someone had also known how to get into the locked cockpit with the special "Boeing key"; perhaps grabbing it off a wounded flight attendant or forcing a crew-member at knifepoint to open the door. Radio and text messages sent from the ground went unanswered. Another attendant, Betty Ong, punched the number 8 of a seatback GTE Airphone and got through to an airlines reservation agent. "She said two flight attendants had been stabbed and a passenger had had his throat slashed," the agent reported. Ong passed on the information that four hijackers who seemed to be Middle Eastern had come from first-class seats 2A, 2B, 9A and 9B. There were in fact five hijackers, led by a man who at 8:33 A.M. made another announcement, calmly and politely, to the passengers and the controllers below. "Nobody move, please. We are going back to the airport. Do not try to make any stupid moves."

Madeline Sweeney's voice on the mobile phone was now a scream. "I see water and buildings—oh my God, oh my God!" Minutes later Flight 11 sliced into the North Tower of the World Trade Center on the tip of Manhattan. A documentary-maker, filming with the New York Fire Brigade in the street below, raised his camera instinctively as he heard the plane roar overhead. He recorded the moment of impact as the huge machine crashed at five hundred miles an hour into the wall of glass and steel, mushrooming out in a cloud of fire.

Thousands of miles south, in Florida, the President of the United States was arriving at a school in Sarasota to take part in a reading session with the children. A senior aide brought George W. Bush news of what seemed to be an accident involving a small twin-engined plane. "This is pilot error," the President recalled saying. "The guy must have had a heart attack."

Four minutes before Flight 11 hit the World Trade Center, a pilot on a second plane out of Boston, United Airlines Flight 175 to Los Angeles, had radioed the control tower in response to an enquiry if he knew Flight 11 was in trouble. Captain Victor Saracini, Flight 175's pilot, confirmed that he had heard something which indicated a problem with the earlier plane. "We heard a suspicious transmission on our departure from Boston," said the captain. "Sounds like someone keyed the mike and said, 'Everyone stay in your seats.'"

Within ninety seconds Flight 175 itself, with nine crew and fifty-six passengers aboard, suddenly veered from its course over northern New Jersey, moving south before making a U-turn to the north, towards New York City. Again the transponder was shut off.

At 8:50 the manager of United Airlines' systems operations centre in Chicago received a call from a maintenance mechanic. He had been called by a woman, who screamed, "Oh my God, the crew has been killed, a female flight attendant has been stabbed—we've been hijacked!" before the line went dead.

Across the water from the World Trade Center, a couple in an apartment had set up their video camera to film the smoking North Tower. At 9:03 the camera caught Flight 175 heading swiftly and unerringly, like a dart, for the second skyscraper, the South Tower. On the audio track the screams of the woman sear that moment in the memory: "Oh my God, oh my God, oh Holy Jesus . . . " repeated over and over as the spray of burning aviation fuel and debris rain from the sky.

Sitting on a stool amid the schoolchildren in Sarasota, a camera also caught the face of George W. Bush as he was told about the second plane. The President's features froze into a mask, but his eyes showed the disbelief and the horror as the White House Chief of Staff whispered in his ear, "A second plane hit the second tower; America is under attack." Bush later recalled clearly what went through his mind in that instant: "They had declared war on us and I made up my mind at that moment that we were going to war," he told the *Washington Post*. "Really good," the President said to the children still reading around him as he excused himself and left the room. At 9:30 he appeared before the television cameras outside to announce "terrorism will not stand," an echo of the words used by his father eleven years before. "This will not stand," George Bush senior had said when Iraq invaded Kuwait in 1990. It was a supreme irony that these words prompted the deployment of U.S. forces to the Gulf, an act which Osama bin Laden would use to justify his reign of terror against America.

In Washington George Tenet, the Director of the CIA, was breakfasting at the St. Regis hotel with an old friend, ex-Senator David Boren. The "chatter" in the intelligence system over the summer, the sense that something big was about to happen, at last made sense. "This has Bin Laden all over it. I've got to go," Tenet said to Boren. "I wonder if this has anything to do with that guy taking pilot training," the CIA Director mused, referring to a French-Moroccan, Zacharias Moussaoui, who had been detained just weeks before after attracting attention at a Minnesota jet training facility.

Ten minutes before Flight 175 hit the World Trade Center another plane, American Airlines Flight 77, bound from Dulles airport near Washington to Los Angeles, also stopped responding to radio calls. At 8:56 AM the Boeing 757, with six crew and fifty-eight passengers aboard, had its flight transponder turned off and no one could raise the pilot, Charles Burlingame. Among the people on board was Barbara Olson, a frequent commentator on CNN and the wife of Theodore Olson, the U.S. Solicitor General. Mr. Olson was in his office when his secretary told him his wife was on the phone. "She said the hijackers had box-cutters and knives—they rounded up the passengers and the two pilots at the back of the plane," said Theodore Olson. He told his wife about the Trade Center crashes. "What should I tell the pilot?" his wife asked. She was cut off and her husband alerted the Justice Department command centre to the hijacking. Mrs. Olson called back and said the plane was circling, then moving north-east.

Secret Service agents burst into the West Wing office of the White House, startling the Vice-President, Dick Cheney, starting work at his desk. "Sir, we have to leave immediately," said one of the agents. Radar showed an aeroplane making for the centre of Washington, D.C.

The ground controllers were finding it hard to track Flight 77 without the transponder but had picked up the aircraft as it crossed the Pentagon building on the edge of the city. They thought it was on autopilot and heading for the White House, but the plane suddenly made a sweeping circle to the right, dropping down low over a traffic-jammed highway. Skimming the roofs of the cars, Flight 77 slammed into the western face of the Pentagon shortly after 9:40 AM.

In the bunker below the White House the instruction went out to the Federal Aviation Authority to land all the 4,546 aircraft that were in the skies above the United States that morning. Fighter planes were scrambled as both combat patrols and to provide an escort for Air Force One, bringing the President to a secure USAF base. The nation was put on "DefCon 3," the highest level of offensive readiness. Bush and Cheney conferred on a secure line and the order was given to shoot down any civilian airliner known to be in the control of hijackers. "I had the television pictures of the World Trade Center before me and a clear understanding that once the plane was hijacked, it was a weapon," said the Vice-President.

United Airlines Flight 93 was forty minutes late that morning leaving Newark airport to fly to San Francisco. It took off at 8:42 instead of at 8:00, as it should have done to play its assigned role in the deadly aerial ballet. The captain was Jason Dahl and there were six other crew members and thirty-seven passengers aboard the Boeing 757. As it flew west into northern Ohio, United Airlines ground control transmitted a system-wide message warning all its pilots of a potential "cockpit intrusion" following the hijacking of Flight 77. The crew on Flight 93 replied by pushing a button that read out "confirmed" to show they had received the message.

On board, passengers began receiving mobile-phone calls from relatives and friends alerting them to the seizure and crashing of the earlier flights. Suddenly, at 9:25, there were two short radio bursts from Flight 93 and ground controllers heard garbled shouting, distorted by the frequency of the signal: "Get out of here, get out of here!" It was followed by a scuffling sound and then an accented voice speaking rapidly.

"Hi, this is the captain," a man said. "We'd like you all to remain seated. There is a bomb on board and we are going to turn back to the airport."

As the radio message was logged on the ground the U.S. military were informed. In the bunker an aide approached the Vice-President: "There is a plane eighty miles out," he said. "There is a fighter in the area, should we engage?"

"Yes," replied Cheney, without hesitation. Later he would tell the *Washington Post* the decision had seemed "painful but nonetheless clear-cut—I didn't agonise over it."

The cockpit recorder on Flight 93 picked up the sound of someone being choked, then voices in Arabic reassuring each other, "Everything is fine." One of the passengers, Tom Burnett, called his wife Deena, who was giving their three children breakfast in San Francisco: "I'm on Flight 93 and we've been hijacked. They've knifed a guy and there's a bomb on board—call the authorities."

In New Jersey Lyzbeth Glick received a call from her husband Jeremy on board Flight 93. He described Middle Eastern-looking men wearing red bandannas round their heads. "I love you," the couple said to each other over and over again. Jeremy asked if it was true what other passengers had heard—that planes had crashed into the World Trade Center. He wondered if that was where Flight 93 was headed. Herded into the back, the passengers were beginning to whisper among themselves. They were thinking of "rushing the hijackers" Glick, a former judo champion, said on the phone to his wife. Did she think it was a good idea? "Go for it," Lyz replied.

Meanwhile flight attendant Sandy Bradshaw called her husband and said there was talk of doing something—she was filling coffee pots with boiling water in readiness. Another passenger, Todd Beamer, was patched through to an Airphone supervisor in Illinois, Lisa Jefferson. He told her two pilots were lying dead or gravely wounded on the floor in the first-class cabin.

Deena Burnett called her husband, Tom, sobbing as she told him another plane had crashed, this time into the Pentagon. "My God," was all he could say. "They seem to be taking planes and driving them into designated landmarks all over the East Coast," said his wife. "It's as if hell has been unleashed."

At 9:36 Flight 93 made a U-turn and started heading back to Washington. As the plane lurched Todd Beamer became agitated and told the phone supervisor they were flying erratically. "We're going down, we're coming back up. We're turning around and going back north," said Beamer. He asked Lisa Jefferson to recite the Lord's Prayer with him. He said he and the others had formed a plan to hit back. "I thought it was pretty dangerous. I asked was he sure he wanted to do that?" said Jefferson. "Todd said at that point he thought that was what he had to do."

Also on board Flight 93 was Donald Greene, an executive of Flight Instrument Corporation and a qualified pilot. The other passengers probably knew of his skills, and felt confident they could get the plane down safely after overpowering the terrorists.

"Are you ready? Let's roll," said Beamer before laying down his phone. Jeremy Glick put his phone to one side too, after telling his wife to take care of their new baby daughter Emmy. "Hang on, I'll be back," he told Lyz. She handed the phone to her father, unable to listen any longer.

The air-traffic controllers kept calling the cockpit, but in vain. Relatives kept vigil by their telephones—the lines were still open, but all they heard was a crackling sound and then silence. At 10:03 Flight 93 crashed in a field south-east of Pittsburgh; a crater forty feet deep bloomed around the wreckage.

On Air Force One President Bush anxiously asked, "Did we shoot it down or did it crash?" Two hours later came the confirmation: the plane had not been shot down by fighter aircraft. "I think an act of heroism occurred on board that plane," Dick Cheney said quietly. The crashing of four American planes and the murder of the 245 innocent people in them was just the beginning of the death and destruction visited on the United States that day.

"Threats and Responses: Pieces of a Puzzle; On Plotters' Path to U.S., a Stop at bin Laden Camp"
By Richard Bernstein with reporting by Douglas Frantz, Don Van Natta Jr., and David Johnston
From the **New York Times**
September 10, 2002

In devising and implementing the September 11 terrorist attacks, Al Qaeda was methodical, patient, and devoted. The initial planning began several years before and relied on the successful completion of many complex steps. Even so, it has been estimated that the entire operation—from planning to execution—ended up costing no more than $300,000. What follows is a piece from the New York Times *written just before the first anniversary of the attacks. In it,* Times *reporter Richard Bernstein reveals the key components of the terrorists' plan and the methodical way in which it was successfully carried out.*

———□———

In October 1999, at the radical Quds mosque in Hamburg, several men attended the wedding of Said Bahaji, a German-

born Muslim of Moroccan descent who is believed to have
been in charge of logistics for the local cell of Al Qaeda.
Looking back, investigators see it as a gathering of the
most important of the Sept. 11 terrorist teams just as the
plotting began.

Among the men at the wedding were Mr. Atta, who was
from a middle-class family in Egypt; Ziad al-Jarrah, who had left
his native Lebanon in April 1996 to fulfill a dream of studying
aeronautical engineering in Europe; and Marwan al-Shehhi, a
citizen of the United Arab Emirates who, also arriving in
Germany in 1996, seems to have been almost inseparable from
Mr. Atta. Investigators believe that the men were at the controls
of three of the four planes that were commandeered on Sept. 11.

Others were at the ceremony as well, men from several
countries who investigators believe were part of the plot's network of support.

Among them, for example, was Mohammed Heidar
Zammar, a German of Moroccan ancestry who is believed to
have recruited for Al Qaeda among the young radical Muslims
who prayed at the Quds mosque. Another was Ramzi bin al-
Shibh of Yemen, a roommate of Mr. Atta in Hamburg and a
man who would most likely have been among the hijackers,
except his repeated applications for visas to the United States
were turned down . . .

In forming a terrorist cell in Hamburg, Mr. Atta and company were doing what radical young Muslims were doing across
the globe, participating in a movement whose chief backer and
inspiration was the renegade Saudi millionaire Osama bin
Laden. A few months before the Bahaji wedding, in February

1998, Mr. bin Laden had issued a well-publicized fatwa, or Muslim religious order, calling on all Muslims to "comply with God's order to kill the Americans and plunder their money wherever and whenever they find it." Then, in August 1998, Al Qaeda succeeded in simultaneous truck bombings of the American embassies in Nairobi and Dar es Salaam, killing 250 people, including 11 Americans, an event that no doubt electrified the members of Al Qaeda cells in other countries.

In addition, Hamburg, and specifically the Quds mosque, was an important center for recruitment into the radical Muslim cause . . .

The presence of all of these men at the wedding of Mr. Bahaji has led investigators to believe that the plan to attack the United States had essentially been formed by then, a bit under two years before Sept. 11, 2001. A videotape of the wedding obtained by German officials shows Mr. bin al-Shibh speaking of the "danger" posed by Jews, and then he recited a paean to jihad, or holy war, against the supposed enemies of Islam.

Soon after the wedding of Mr. Bahaji, who fled Germany after Sept. 11, the men in the Hamburg cell began to take concrete steps to implement a plan. Most important, according to German investigators, all three of the Hamburg hijackers, as well as Mr. bin al-Shibh and Mr. Bahaji, went to Afghanistan for training in an Al Qaeda camp.

Klaus Ulrich Kersten, director of Germany's federal anti-crime agency, the Bundeskriminalamt, said the men were all in Afghanistan from late 1999 until early 2000.

In going to Afghanistan, the members of the Hamburg cell entered into a culture of holy war that was already well established. The Muslim men who journeyed to Afghanistan in order to join Al Qaeda went through a similar, demanding program of basic military training. Those who showed exceptional promise were singled out for special missions, including what were called martyrdom operations, like the 1998 African embassy bombings, or Sept. 11 . . .

When the Hamburg men returned to Germany toward the end of February 2000, they began the first practical steps toward implementing the plot, sending e-mail to request information from 31 flight schools in the United States.

Mr. Nehm, the German prosecutor, described a conversation in which Mr. Shehhi mentioned the World Trade Center to a Hamburg librarian, in April or May 2000, and boasted: "There will be thousands of dead. You will all think of me."

"You will see," Mr. Nehm quoted Mr. Shehhi as saying. "In America something is going to happen. There will be many people killed."

Learning to Fly
A Malaysia Meeting, Then to the U.S.

Two months after the wedding in Hamburg and halfway around the world, a group of seven or eight Muslim militants got together in Kuala Lumpur, Malaysia, at the apartment of a local supporter of Al Qaeda. The C.I.A. had learned of the meeting and tipped off Malaysian intelligence, which secretly photographed it. Two of the men photographed, Khalid al-Midhar and Nawaq Alhazmi, would later be among the 19 hijackers.

Malaysian intelligence had no listening devices planted at the meeting, so it is not clear what its purpose was. The main item on the agenda might have been the plans for an attack on an American naval vessel. One of the men present was later implicated in the attack on the Navy destroyer *Cole*, in October 2000.

But it is possible that the emerging plans for an assault on American territory were also discussed. American officials have said they are not certain that Mr. bin al-Shibh was there, but in recent interviews foreign investigators, who have seen the photographs of the Kuala Lumpur meeting, say they are convinced that he was. Credit card records also indicate that Mr. bin al-Shibh was in Malaysia at the time of the meeting.

The signs are strong that just after the Kuala Lumpur meeting, Mr. Midhar and Mr. Alhazmi became part of the Sept. 11 plan. A few weeks later, in January 2000, the two men became the first of the hijackers to land in the United States, arriving in Los Angeles on a flight from Bangkok. Within weeks, the two had registered at a flight school in San Diego and begun learning to fly—though they showed very little aptitude for it and were soon dropped by the flight instructor.

Why did the plot involve two separate groups, one that prepared in California and one in Florida, where Mr. Atta, Mr. Shehhi and Mr. Jarrah arrived a few months later?

One possibility is that Mr. Midhar and Mr. Alhazmi were better known within Al Qaeda than any of the young men from Hamburg. Intelligence officials say Mr. Midhar's father-in-law ran a safehouse in Yemen that relayed messages between Qaeda leaders and operatives. Qaeda leaders might have wanted the hijackers to enter from two separate tracks for added security. It is also possible that Mr. Midhar and Mr.

Alhazmi were supposed to keep an eye on Mr. Atta from
enough of a distance that they would not arouse the suspicion
of American law enforcement authorities and report on him to
Al Qaeda headquarters in Afghanistan.

At some point, Mr. Midhar and Mr. Alhazmi were joined
by Hani Hanjour, the 29-year-old member of a well-off Saudi
family who is believed to have been the pilot of American
Airlines Flight 77, which was hijacked after taking off from
Dulles International Airport and crashed into the Pentagon.
Mr. Hanjour had been in the United States since 1996, when
he attended a flying school in Scottsdale, Ariz. Despite a poor
record as a student, he was able to get a commercial pilot's
license in 1999.

Mr. Midhar and Mr. Alhazmi settled into San Diego,
attending activities at the local Islamic Center. Mr. Midhar
traveled extensively outside the United States, but Mr. Alhazmi
seems to have stayed put. He even advertised for a wife with
an Arab-language Internet dating service and received two
replies—an odd thing for a man on a suicide mission to do.

The Hamburg group arrived in the United States several
months after the Malaysian group. Mr. Shehhi was first, arriving in Newark on May 29. Mr. Atta came on June 3, also
through Newark, but in another of the unresolved mysteries he
arrived via Prague, where he took considerable trouble to go.
He first went to Prague via plane but was turned away because
he did not have a valid visa. He went back to Germany on the
first flight, obtained a visa in Bonn and then returned to Prague
by bus. He stayed just one night and left for the United States
the next day.

Several weeks later, on June 27, Mr. Jarrah arrived in Atlanta on a flight from Munich.

Within a few weeks of their arrival, all three undertook the first task of the plot: they took flying lessons at various academies, getting their licenses around the end of 2000. After learning how to fly small planes, each paid for time on a simulator learning the techniques of flying larger planes, specifically wide-bodied Boeing passenger jets . . .

The Muscle Arrives
13 Saudis Join the Plot Leaders

When Mr. Atta returned to Florida from Spain on July 19 the plot swung into its final phase. Over the next several weeks, 13 men, all Saudis, entered the country on valid visas to join Mr. Atta, the three other pilots and Mr. Alhazmi and Mr. Midhar.

The 13 came to provide muscle for the plot—to help execute the hijackings and keep passengers and crew at bay while the newly trained pilots flew the jets to their targets. It seems likely that the Saudis were among the legions of young Muslim men who went to Afghanistan in response to the call to make holy war against the enemies of Islam . . .

Last Details
Bank Accounts, ID's, Rentals, Plane Tickets

In the final few weeks before the attacks, the 19 men busied themselves with practical details. Many of the Saudis opened bank accounts at the Sun Trust Bank. They got driver's licenses, thereby satisfying the airlines' requirement that all passengers show government-issued photo ID's before boarding a plane. Several of the men got Virginia identification cards via a black market that operated out of a parking lot in Arlington. To maintain discipline and to stay in good condition, most of the men got temporary memberships in health clubs in Florida.

Over the course of the summer, the various teams went to separate places on the East Coast. One took up residence at motels in Laurel, Md., not far from Dulles. Several men rented an apartment in Paterson, N.J., just across the river from Manhattan where they had distant views of their main target, the World Trade Center. Others, including Mr. Atta, continued to live in Florida.

Airline, rental car, and cellphone records show that Mr. Atta was furiously busy. He rented cars often and put thousands of miles on them. American officials say he also made regular trips from Florida to Newark, presumably to meet with the group in Paterson. Because some of those living in Paterson had come across the country from California, it may have been on one of these trips that the Florida group and the California group began to coordinate their plans directly. The F.B.I. has also noticed spikes in cellphone use at what seem to be critical points in the plan; for example, just after the arrest of Mr. Moussaoui and just before the men began, in late August, to buy tickets for the flights they would hijack.

Investigators found that members of both the Florida and California teams were in Las Vegas in August, and they believe that final plans might have been coordinated then, including, quite possibly, what flights to hijack and which team members would be on which flight. As Sept. 11 neared, the teams were geographically in place. The men who hijacked Flight 77 from Dulles were installed in Laurel. Those who seized United Airlines Flight 93 were at hotels near Newark. Most of the 10 who hijacked two planes at Logan International Airport were at a hotel in downtown Boston.

In one of the most mysterious aspects of the plot, Mr. Atta and one of the Saudi recruits, Abdulaziz Alomari, drove to Portland, Me., on the night of Sept. 10. The two stayed in a motel in Portland and took an early morning commuter flight to Boston the next day. In doing so, they took a risk. They did not have much time to make the connection from their commuter flight to United Airlines Flight 11, the flight they commandeered. Indeed, the connection was so close that, had the commuter flight been at all late, they would have missed the very flight they intended to hijack, even as their confederates coming from downtown Boston were already assembled at Logan.

There have been many theories about this: that they made contact with an accomplice in Portland who gave them the final go-ahead; or more likely that by arriving on a connecting flight, they would avoid the security check in Boston. The explanations seem unsatisfactory, given the risk and especially given that only Mr. Atta and Mr. Alomari, who were on the same hijacking team, took the steps they did, which means that whatever their motivation, it did not apply to the three other teams.

Perhaps the best explanation is that Mr. Atta saw arriving on a connecting flight in Boston as a kind of insurance policy. Assuming that security procedures were less rigorous at a smaller airport, he may have believed that he and Mr. Alomari had a better chance of getting their knives through the checkpoint than in Boston. That would mean that, even if all the other team members failed in their assigned tasks, at least Mr. Atta and one confederate would succeed in theirs.

It was perhaps a final measure of Mr. Atta's determination and fanaticism. If the plot succeeded only in hijacking one plane and flying it to its target, he wanted to be sure that it was the plane he was on.

On the last night, the hijackers were supposed to read some handwritten instructions that Mr. Atta had distributed. The instructions told the men to shave excess hair from their bodies, to read certain passages of the Koran and to remember that the most beautiful virgins, "the women of paradise," awaited the martyrs of Islam. "When the confrontation begins," the instructions continued, "strike like champions who do not want to go back to this world."

The men who waited to strike and to die were near the end of a long journey. Mr. Atta had gone from Cairo to Hamburg to Afghanistan to the Czech Republic to Switzerland to Spain and, of course, to the United States. Others came from Saudi Arabia, Yemen, Lebanon, the United Arab Emirates; they had passed through Malaysia, Thailand and states of the Persian Gulf on their way to what would come to be called Ground Zero.

There the complex plot to murder Americans in fulfillment of Osama bin Laden's fatwa "to kill the Americans and their allies" would take its terrible toll on thousands of unsuspecting men and women who got up on Sept. 11 to go

to work or to travel on airplanes and who died before the
morning was over.

"The City and the Pillars"
By Adam Gopnik
From **The New Yorker**
September 24, 2001

*In this piece, written less than a week after the attack upon
the World Trade Center, author and regular* New Yorker *contributor Adam Gopnik attempts to capture the fragile emotions
of the city in the immediate aftermath of September 11. The
attacks were so sudden and so shocking that people had no
chance to wrap their minds around the sheer enormity of the
moment. Everyone responded in different ways. Some
shopped. Some hoarded supplies. Others simply walked the
suddenly altered streets of the city that they thought they had
known so well. It will be impossible for any New Yorker to
forget the surreal nature of that first day. Adam Gopnik perfectly captures the day's hazy disorientation. Yet he also seeks
to examine how the destruction of the Twin Towers made more
obvious the gulf separating the symbolic and iconic New York
and the "real" city—the shaken but still standing city of side-
walks and grocery stores and public schools and everyday
lives. New York represents so much to so many people. It car-
ries such distinct, almost mythic associations, borrowed from
film, photography, literature, and painting. At the same time,
however, it is also a place of daily life, where people go about
their mundane business just as they do in any other village or*

town. Now that the city's most recognizable symbol has been destroyed, the "real" New York—New York as it is lived and experienced—seems exposed and vulnerable. Inevitably, however, the city will regain its brash confidence and sense of strength and iconic New York will again exist side-by-side with the everyday city that is home to millions.

———□———

On the morning of the day they did it, the city was as beautiful as it had ever been. Central Park had never seemed so gleaming and luxuriant—the leaves just beginning to fall, and the light on the leaves left on the trees somehow making them at once golden and bright green. A bird-watcher in the Ramble made a list of the birds he saw there, from the northern flicker and the red-eyed vireo to the rose-breasted grosbeak and the Baltimore oriole. "Quite a few migrants around today," he noted happily.

In some schools, it was the first day, and children went off as they do on the first day, with the certainty that, this year, we will have fun again. The protective bubble that for the past decade or so had settled over the city, with a bubble's transparency and bright highlights, still seemed to be in place above us. We always knew that that bubble would burst, but we imagined it bursting as bubbles do: no one will be hurt, we thought, or they will be hurt only as people are hurt when bubbles burst, a little soap in your mouth. It seemed safely in place for another day as the children walked to school. The stockbroker fathers delivered—no, inserted—their kids into school as they always do, racing downtown, their cell phones already at work, like cartoons waiting for their usual morning caption: "Exasperated at 8 A.M."

A little while later, a writer who happened to be downtown saw a flock of pigeons rise, high and fast, and thought, Why are the pigeons rising? It was only seconds before he realized that the pigeons had felt the wave of the concussion before he heard the sound. In the same way, the shock wave hit us before the sound, the image before our understanding. For the lucky ones, the day from then on was spent in a strange, calm, and soul-emptying back and forth between the impossible images on television and the usual things on the street.

Around noon, a lot of people crowded around a lamppost on Madison, right underneath a poster announcing the Wayne Thiebaud show at the Whitney: all those cakes, as if to signal the impotence of our abundance. The impotence of our abundance! In the uptown supermarkets, people began to shop. It was a hoarding instinct, of course, though oddly not brought on by any sense of panic; certainly no one on television or radio was suggesting that people needed to hoard. Yet people had the instinct to do it, and, in any case, in New York the instinct to hoard quickly seemed to shade over into the instinct to consume, shop for anything, shop because it might be a comfort. One woman emerged from a Gristede's on Lexington with a bottle of olive oil and said, "I had to get something." Mostly people bought water—bottled water, French and Italian—and many people, waiting in the long lines, had Armageddon baskets: the Manhattan version, carts filled with steaks, Häagen-Dazs, and butter. Many of the carts held the goods of the bubble decade, hothouse goods: flavored balsamics and cappellini and arugula. There was no logic to it, as one man pointed out in that testy, superior, patient tone: "If trucks can't get through, the Army will take over and give everybody K rations or some crazy thing; if they do, this won't matter." Someone asked him what was he doing uptown? He had been down there, got out before the building collapsed, and walked up.

People seemed not so much to suspend the rituals of normalcy as to carry on with them in a kind of bemusement— as though to reject the image on the screen, as though to say, That's there, we're here, they're not here yet, it's not here yet. "Everything turns away quite leisurely from the disaster," Auden wrote, about a painting of Icarus falling from the sky; now we know why they turned away—they saw the boy falling from the sky, sure enough, but they did not know what to do about it. If we do the things we know how to do, New Yorkers thought, then what has happened will matter less.

The streets and parks were thinned of people, but New York is so dense—an experiment in density, really, as Venice is an experiment in water—that the thinning just produced the normal density of Philadelphia or Baltimore. It added to the odd calm. "You wouldn't put it in a book," a young man with an accent said to a girl in the Park, and then he added, "Do you like to ski?" Giorgio Armani was in the Park—Giorgio Armani? Yes, right behind the Metropolitan Museum, with his entourage, beautiful Italian boys and girls in tight white T-shirts. "Cinema," he kept saying, his hands moving back and forth like an accordion player's. "Cinema."

Even urban geography is destiny, and New York, a long thin island, cuts downtown off from uptown, west side off from east. (And a kind of moral miniaturization is always at work, as we try unconsciously to seal ourselves from the disaster:

people in Europe say "America attacked" and people in America say "New York attacked" and people in New York think, Downtown attacked.) For the financial community, this was the Somme; it was impossible not to know someone inside that building, or thrown from it. Whole companies, tiny civilizations, an entire Zip Code vanished. Yet those of us outside that world, hovering in midtown, were connected to the people dying in the towers only by New York's uniquely straight lines of sight—you looked right down Fifth Avenue and saw that strange, still neat package of white smoke.

The city has never been so clearly, so surreally, sectioned as it became on Wednesday and Thursday. From uptown all the way down to Fourteenth Street, life is almost entirely normal—fewer cars, perhaps, one note quieter on the street, but children and moms and hot-dog venders on nearly every corner. In the flower district, the wholesalers unpack autumn branches from the boxes they arrived in this morning. "That came over the bridge?" someone asks, surprised at the thought of a truck driver waiting patiently for hours just to bring in blossoming autumn branches. The vender nods.

At Fourteenth Street, one suddenly enters the zone of the missing, of mourning not yet acknowledged. It is, in a way, almost helpful to walk in that strange new village, since the concussion wave of fear that has been sucking us in since Tuesday is replaced with an outward ripple of grief and need, something human to hold on to. The stanchions and walls are plastered with homemade color-Xerox posters, smiling snapshots above, a text below, searching for the missing: "Roger Mark Rasweiler. Missing. One WTC, 100th floor." "We Need

Your Help: Giovanna 'Gennie' Gambale." "We're Looking for Kevin M. Williams, 104th Fl. WTC." "Have You Seen Him? Robert 'Bob' Dewitt." "Ed Feldman—Call Ross." "Millan Rustillo—Missing WTC." Every lost face is smiling, caught at Disney World or Miami Beach, on vacation. Every poster lovingly notes the missing person's height and weight to the last ounce and inch. "Clown tattoo on right shoulder," one says. On two different posters there is an apologetic note along with the holiday snap: "Was Not Wearing Sunglasses on Tuesday."

Those are the ones who've gone missing. On television, the reporters keep talking about the World Trade Center as a powerful symbol of American financial power. And yet it was, in large part, the back office of Wall Street. As Eric Darton showed in his fine social history of the towers, they were less a symbol of America's financial might than a symbol of the Port Authority's old inferiority complex. It was not the citadel of capitalism but, according to the real order of things in the capitalist world, just a come-on—a desperate scheme dreamed up in the late fifties to bring businesses back downtown. In later years, of course, downtown New York became the center of world trade, for reasons that basically had nothing to do with the World Trade Center, so that now Morgan Stanley and Cantor Fitzgerald were there, but for a long time it was also a big state office building, where you went to get a document stamped or a license renewed. No one loved it save children, who took to it because it was iconically so simple, so tall and two. When a child tried to draw New York, he would draw the simplest available icons: two rectangles and an airplane going by them.

Near Washington Square, the streets empty out, and the square itself is beautiful again. "I saw it coming," a bicycle messenger says. "I thought it was going to take off the top of that building." He points to the little Venetian-style campanile on Washington Square South. The Village seems like a village. In a restaurant on Washington Place at ten-thirty, the sous-chefs are quietly prepping for lunch, with the chairs still on all the tables and the front door open and unguarded. "We're going to try and do dinner today," one of the chefs says. A grown woman rides a scooter down the middle of LaGuardia Place. Several café owners, or workers, go through the familiar act of hosing down the sidewalk. With the light pall of smoke hanging over everything, this everyday job becomes somehow cheering, cleansing. If you enter one of the open cafés and order a meal, the familiar dialogue—"And a green salad with that." "You mean a side salad?" "Yeah, that'd be fine. . . . What kind of dressing do you have?"—feels reassuring, too, another calming routine.

Houston Street is the dividing line, the place where the world begins to end. In SoHo, there is almost no one on the street. No one is allowed on the streets except residents, and they are hidden in their lofts. Nothing is visible, except the cloud of white smoke and soot that blows from the dense stillness below Canal. An art critic and a museum curator watched the explosions from right here. "It was a sound like two trucks crashing on Canal, no louder than that, than something coming by terribly fast, and the building was struck," the critic said. "I thought, This is it, mate, the nuclear attack, I'm going to die. I was peaceful about it, though. But then the flame subsided, and then the building fell." The critic and the curator watched it fall together. Decades had passed in that neighborhood where people insisted that now everything was spectacle, nothing had meaning. Now there was a spectacle, and it meant.

The smell, which fills the empty streets of SoHo from Houston to Canal, blew uptown on Wednesday night, and is not entirely horrible from a reasonable distance—almost like the smell of smoked mozzarella, a smell of the bubble time. Closer in, it becomes acrid, and unbreathable. The white particulate smoke seems to wreathe the empty streets—to wrap right around them. The authorities call this the "frozen zone." In the "Narrative of A. Gordon Pym," spookiest and most cryptic of Poe's writings, a man approaches the extremity of existence, the pole beneath the Southern Pole. "The whole ashy material fell now continually around us," he records in his diary, "and in vast quantities. The range of vapor to the southward had arisen prodigiously in the horizon, and began to assume more distinctness of form. I can liken it to nothing but a limitless cataract, rolling silently into the sea from some immense and far-distant rampart in the heaven. The gigantic curtain ranged along the whole extent of the southern horizon. It emitted no sound." Poe, whose house around here was torn down not long ago, is a realist now.

More than any other city, New York exists at once as a city of symbols and associations, literary and artistic, and as a city of real things. This is an emotional truth, of course— New York is a city of wacky dreams and of disillusioning realities. But it is also a plain, straightforward architectural truth, a visual truth, a material truth. The city looks one

way from a distance, a skyline full of symbols, inviting pil-
grims and Visigoths, and another way up close, a city full of
people. The Empire State and Chrysler Buildings exist as
symbols of thirties materialism and as abstract ideas of skyscrapers and as big dowdy office buildings—a sign and then
a thing and then a sign and then a thing and then a sign,
going back and forth all the time. (It is possible to transact
business in the Empire State Building, and only then nudge
yourself and think, Oh, yeah, this is the Empire State
Building.) The World Trade Center existed both as a thrilling
double exclamation point at the end of the island and as a
rotten place to have to go and get your card stamped, your
registration renewed.

The pleasure of living in New York has always been the
pleasure of living in both cities at once: the symbolic city of
symbolic statements (this is big, I am rich, get me) and the
everyday city of necessities, MetroCards and coffee shops
and long waits and longer trudges. On the afternoon of that
day, the symbolic city, the city that the men in the planes had
attacked, seemed much less important than the real city,
where the people in the towers lived. The bubble is gone, but
the city beneath—naked now in a new way, not startling but
vulnerable—seemed somehow to increase in our affection,
our allegiance. On the day they did it, New Yorkers walked
the streets without, really, any sense of "purpose" or "pride"
but with the kind of tender necessary patriotism that lies in
just persisting.

New York, E. B. White wrote in 1949, holds a steady,
irresistible charm for perverted dreamers of destruction,

because it seems so impossible. "The intimation of mortality is part of New York now," he went on to write, "in the sound of jets overhead." We have heard the jets now, and we will probably never be able to regard the city with quite the same exasperated, ironic affection we had for it before. Yet on the evening of the day, one couldn't walk through Central Park, or down Seventh Avenue, or across an empty but hardly sinister Times Square—past the light on the trees, or the kids on their scooters, or the people sitting worried in the outdoor restaurants with menus, frowning, as New Yorkers always do, as though they had never seen a menu before—without feeling a surprising rush of devotion to the actual New York, Our Lady of the Subways, New York as it is. It is the symbolic city that draws us here, and the real city that keeps us. It seems hard but important to believe that that city will go on, because we now know what it would be like to lose it, and it feels like losing life itself.

CHAPTER TWO

PEOPLE, PLACES, AND ENVIRONMENTS: COMMUNITY IN THE WAKE OF SEPTEMBER 11

Here Is New York
By E. B. White
1949

E. B. White, best known for his classic children's book Charlotte's Web, *has produced some of the most accomplished and evocative writings on the city of New York. After moving to the city from Seattle in 1924 (he grew up in upstate New York), he soon began writing about the fascinating dynamism of the metropolis with which he quickly fell in love. Working for the* New Yorker, *E. B. White wrote this selection in 1949, almost twenty years before construction began on the World Trade Center. While the sociological insights of the essay remain largely true, White's prophesying about the extreme vulnerability of New York is even more on target and, in the wake of September 11, chilling. At the dawn of the atomic age and with the memory of the devastating bombing of European and Japanese cities during World War II (1939–1945) still fresh in his mind, White may have been afraid that New York could someday become a similar target,*

and the city he knew and loved could be destroyed. The two
planes that crashed into the World Trade Center proved that
his worst fears were justified.

———□———

New York is nothing like Paris; it is nothing like London;
and it is not Spokane multiplied by sixty, or Detroit multiplied by four. It is by all odds the loftiest of cities. It even
managed to reach the highest point in the sky at the lowest
moment of the depression. The Empire State Building shot
twelve hundred and fifty feet into the air when it was mad-
ness to put out as much as six inches of new growth. (The
building has a mooring mast that no dirigible has ever tied
to; it employs a man to flush toilets in slack times; it has
been hit by an airplane in a fog, struck countless times by
lightning, and been jumped off of by so many unhappy people
that pedestrians instinctively quicken step when passing
Fifth Avenue and 34th Street.)

Manhattan has been compelled to expand skyward
because of the absence of any other direction in which to grow.
This, more than any other thing, is responsible for its physical
majesty. It is to the nation what the white church spire is to
the village—the visible symbol of aspiration and faith, the
white plume saying that the way is up. The summer traveler
swings in over Hell Gate Bridge and from the window of his
sleeping car as it glides above the pigeon lofts and back yards
of Queens looks southwest to where the morning light first
strikes the steel peaks of midtown, and he sees its upward
thrust unmistakable: the great walls and towers rising, the

smoke rising, the heat not yet rising, the hopes and ferments of so many awakening millions rising—this vigorous spear that presses heaven hard.

It is a miracle that New York works at all. The whole thing is implausible. Every time the residents brush their teeth, millions of gallons of water must be drawn from the Catskills and the hills of Westchester. When a young man in Manhattan writes a letter to his girl in Brooklyn, the love message gets blown to her through a pneumatic tube— pfft—just like that. The subterranean system of telephone cables, power lines, steam pipes, gas mains, and sewer pipes is reason enough to abandon the island to the gods and the weevils. Every time an incision is made in the pavement, the noisy surgeons expose ganglia that are tangled beyond belief. By rights New York should have destroyed itself long ago, from panic or fire or rioting or failure of some vital supply line in its circulatory system or from some deep labyrinthine short circuit. Long ago the city should have experienced an insoluble traffic snarl at some impossible bottleneck. It should have perished of hunger when food lines failed for a few days. It should have been wiped out by a plague starting in its slums or carried in by ships' rats. It should have been overwhelmed by the sea that licks at it on every side. The workers in its myriad cells should have succumbed to nerves, from the fearful pall of smoke-fog that drifts over every few days from Jersey, blotting out all light at noon and leaving the high offices suspended, men groping and depressed, and the sense of world's end. It should have been touched in the head by the August heat and gone off its rocker.

Mass hysteria is a terrible force, yet New Yorkers seem always to escape it by some tiny margin: they sit in stalled subways without claustrophobia, they extricate themselves from panic situations by some lucky wisecrack, they meet confusion and congestion with patience and grit—a sort of perpetual muddling through. Every facility is inadequate—the hospitals and schools and playgrounds are overcrowded, the express highways are feverish, the unimproved highways and bridges are bottlenecks; there is not enough air and not enough light, and there is usually either too much heat or too little. But the city makes up for its hazards and its deficiencies by supplying its citizens with massive doses of a supplementary vitamin— the sense of belonging to something unique, cosmopolitan, mighty, and unparalleled . . .

The subtlest change in New York is something people don't speak much about but that is in everyone's mind. The city, for the first time in its long history, is destructible. A single flight of planes no bigger than a wedge of geese can quickly end this island fantasy, burn the towers, crumble the bridges, turn the underground passages into lethal chambers, cremate the millions. The intimation of mortality is part of New York now: in the sound of jets overhead, in the black headlines of the latest edition.

All dwellers in cities must live with the stubborn fact of annihilation; in New York the fact is somewhat more concentrated because of the concentration of the city itself, and because, of all targets, New York has a certain clear priority. In the mind of whatever perverted dreamer might loose the lightning, New York must hold a steady, irresistible charm.

It used to be that the Statue of Liberty was the signpost that proclaimed New York and translated it for all the world. Today Liberty shares the role with Death. Along the East River, from the razed slaughterhouses of Turtle Bay, as though in a race with the spectral flight of planes, men are carving out the permanent headquarters of the United Nations—the greatest housing project of them all. In its stride, New York takes on one more interior city, to shelter, this time, all governments, and to clear the slum called war. New York is not a capital city—it is not a national capital or a state capital. But it is by way of becoming the capital of the world . . .

This race—this race between the destroying planes and the struggling Parliament of Man—it sticks in all our heads. The city at last perfectly illustrates both the universal dilemma and the general solution, this riddle in steel and stone is at once the perfect target and the perfect demonstration of nonviolence, of racial brotherhood, this lofty target scraping the skies and meeting the destroying planes halfway, home of all people and all nations, capital of everything, housing the deliberations by which the planes are to be stayed and their errand forestalled.

A block or two west of the new City of Man in Turtle Bay there is an old willow tree that presides over an interior garden. It is a battered tree, long suffering and much climbed, held together by strands of wire but beloved of those who know it. In a way it symbolizes the city: life under difficulties, growth against odds, sap-rise in the midst of concrete, and the steady reaching for the sun. Whenever I look at it nowadays, and feel the cold shadow of the planes, I think: "This must be saved, this particular thing, this very tree." If it were to go, all would go—this city, this mischievous and marvelous monument which not to look upon would be like death.

American Ground: Unbuilding the World Trade Center
By William Langewiesche
2003

In the immediate aftermath of the collapse of the World Trade Center, thousands of volunteers flocked to the disaster scene to help search for the wounded. In the next few days, it became increasingly clear that the search for survivors was really a search for corpses. Even this grim recovery effort, however, would yield little. The destruction of the towers was so complete that relatively few bodies were found. The recovery and salvage effort was performed by many different people. Firefighters, police officers, and construction workers, many of whom were volunteers from around the country, carted off hundreds of thousands of tons of twisted metal and shattered cement. William Langewiesche, author and longtime contributor to the Atlantic Monthly, *spent many days at Ground Zero and recorded his experiences in a controversial book,* American Ground: Unbuilding the World Trade Center. *With the book he made several enemies by revealing the darker*

side of the newly minted American heroes, yet his story
remains a tribute to a community formed in the wake of
tragedy and existing in the very center of hell.

———□———

When the Twin Towers collapsed, on the warm, bright morning
of September 11, 2001, they made a sound heard variously
around New York as a roar, a growl, or distant thunder. The
South Tower was the first to go. At 9:59 its upper floors tilted
briefly before dropping, disintegrating, and driving the building
straight down to the ground. The fall lasted ten seconds, as did
the sound. Many people died, but mercifully fast. Twenty-nine
minutes later the North Tower collapsed just as quickly, and
with much the same result. Somehow a few people survived. For
an instant, each tower left its imprint in the air, a phantom of
pulverized concrete marking a place that then became a memory.
Prefabricated sections of the external steel columns tumbled
down onto lesser buildings, piling onto terraces and rooftops,
punching through parking structures, offices, and stores, induc-
ing secondary collapses and igniting fires. The most catastrophic
effects were eerily selective: with the exception of Saint
Nicholas, a tiny Greek Orthodox church that dissolved in the
rain of steel, the only buildings completely wrecked were those
that carried the World Trade Center label. There were seven in
all, and ultimately none of them endured. Not even the so-called
World Trade Center Seven, a relatively new forty-seven-floor
tower that stood independently across the street from the complex, was able to escape the fate associated with its name.
Though it did not seem seriously wounded at first, it burned

persistently throughout the day, and that evening became the first steel-frame high-rise in history to fall solely because of fire.

There was wider damage, of course, and on the scale of ordinary disasters it was heavy. For thirty years the Twin Towers had stood above the streets as all tall buildings do, as a bomb of sorts, a repository for the prodigious energy originally required to raise so much weight so high. Now, in a single morning, in twin ten-second pulses, the towers released that energy back into the city. Massive steel beams flew through the neighborhood like gargantuan spears, penetrating subway lines and underground passages to depths of thirty feet, crushing them, rupturing water mains and gas lines, and stabbing high into the sides of nearby office towers, where they lodged. The phone system, the fiber-optic network, and the electric power grid were knocked out. Ambulances, cars, and fire trucks were smashed flat by falling debris, and some were hammered five floors down from the street into the insane turmoil erupting inside the World Trade Center's immense "bathtub"—a ten-acre foundation hole, seventy feet deep, that was suffering unimaginable violence as it absorbed the brunt of each tower's collapse . . .

One of the many astonishments of that day is that the building [the South Tower] was able to swallow an entire 767, and to slow it from 590 mph to a stop in merely 209 feet. According to calculations based on photographic evidence of the damaged perimeter, the structure had redistributed the gravity loads so efficiently that only twenty feet from the entry wound the demands being made on intact columns were hardly higher than normal. The building was certainly not safe. It had suffered serious if unknowable damage to the east side of the core. At the same time, for seventy feet along the inside of the south face, and perhaps a short distance along the east face, the floors had been torn loose from the structure, leaving perimeter columns unbraced under the gravity load of the roughly thirty-story building overhead. Still, if not exactly shrugging off the hit, the South Tower had absorbed it well: absent an earthquake or a strong windstorm, the building would have remained standing indefinitely.

But then, of course, there was the fire. As the airplane disintegrated, it released its fuel—roughly 10,000 gallons of volatile "Jet A" kerosene that sprayed and vaporized through the six floors of wreckage, poured into the elevator shafts, shot through broken windows along the north and east faces, and immediately ignited. Apocalyptic though it seemed, the huge fireball that blossomed over the plaza was actually to the building's advantage, because it consumed as much as a third of the available fuel, releasing the heat harmlessly into the air. That left two thirds of the fuel inside the tower, however, and it was widely spread and burning.

The building's sprinkler system had been destroyed by the impact, but in any case it would have lacked the pressure to operate effectively over such a wide area. More significant, much of the light spray-on fireproofing that coated the structural steel had been knocked away—and precisely in the same east-side areas that had sustained the worst damage and now were threatened by unusual and increased loads. On only one of these floors had a fireproofing upgrade that doubled the thickness of the coating been completed—a circumstance that provided for healthy debates afterward, though there was never direct evidence that the thicker fireproofing would have better endured the impact.

At any thickness, the coating was meant to insulate the steel and prevent it from overheating in a fire for at least two hours (by which time an office fire will typically have burned itself out in any given part of a building). The problem with overheating is that long before steel melts, it weakens. In structural steel like that of the South Tower the weakening begins around 3,500 degrees Fahrenheit. By 1,100 degrees the steel loses about half its strength. Kerosene burns twice that hot inside the carefully crafted furnace of an airliner's engine, but within the imperfect combustion chambers of the South Tower impact zone it is thought to have reached at most only about 1,500°—a temperature unlikely to induce the failure of such a tremendously redundant design, especially on a gentle, windless day. Moreover, the kerosene fire simply did not last long enough at any temperature to overheat the building's massive columns. Corley's [W. Gene Corley, lead investigator of the WTC collapse] fire specialists believed that the jet fuel never collected into deep, slow-burning pools, and that it burned through entirely within four minutes. They concluded that jet fuel itself did not bring the tower down.

What it did do, however, was set off raging office fires simultaneously in six different floors. It was a conflagration that would have been impossible for the firemen to control, had they gotten to it—a fire large enough to create its own powerful winds, sucking oxygen in through all the perimeter holes and broken windows, generating energy three to five times greater than that of a standard nuclear power plant, and eventually heating the steel to temperatures as high as 2,000°. The fire fed on wrecked office furniture, computers, carpets, and aircraft cargo, but primarily it fed on ordinary papers—an ample supply of the white sheets that were so much a part of the larger battlefield scene. Without that paper, Corley's experts believed, the fire might not have achieved the intensity necessary to weaken the steel beyond its critical threshold. It would be simplifying things, but not by much, to conclude that it was paperwork that brought the South Tower down.

On the debris pile in the northeast corner the fire melted the remnants of the shattered airliner, which half an hour after entering the building began to flow in a stream of molten aluminum down the tower's outside. Still the tower endured. But then the southeast corner of the eightieth floor collapsed, triggering the progressive failure of the floor along the entire east side of the building. Dust plumes shot out through the broken windows. The eastern perimeter columns now stood unbraced for the space of at least two floors, adding to the dangers that the building already faced from the unbraced condition on the perimeter on the south side. Shortly afterward, in the southeast corner, near the entry wound, a cluster of exterior columns began to buckle. It was 9:59 exactly, merely fifty-six minutes after the airplane hit. Peter Rinaldi [a Port Authority engineer and general manager of the Ground

Zero site] was living the last four seconds of his earlier life. Frank Lombardi [the Port Authority's chief engineer] was pushing into the hotel bar somewhere far below. With its support giving way beneath it, the top of the tower tilted east and then south, rotating in a clockwise direction, and suddenly slammed down. Even if it had been felled from below, the tower could not have capsized in a conventional sense, because like most other buildings, it lacked the structure to hang together for more than a few degrees off vertical. But it was not felled from below; it was hammered from above, and it accelerated as it fell, crushing the core and peeling back the exoskeleton with each successive floor. As the external walls peeled, they broke primarily at the bolted connections, allowing welded prefabricated sections of the columns to fall free. The upper sections fell east and south, and hit the Bankers Trust building; the lower sections fell north and west, and gave the Marriott hotel the first of its two fatal blows.

The North Tower died a half hour after its twin, but because it showed fewer symptoms, less is known about its end. The attack it suffered was similar. It came from another 767, American Flight 11, which was light on passengers and fuel, and flying 100 mph slower than the United flight, though still very fast. The initial impact involved a full, clean entry, almost perfectly centered. The airplane sliced through thirty-six of sixty-one columns on the north face, tore through four floors, and slammed squarely against the weak axis of the core. It took out all three stairwells, destroyed the sprinkler system, knocked the fireproofing from the steel, and blew a piece of landing gear and a fireball through the far wall. Lifejackets and parts of the seats ended up on the roof of the Bankers Trust building. The North Tower swayed, the jet fuel was rapidly consumed, and a terrible office fire broke out.

There were differences, too. The North Tower had the advantage of getting hit high up, thereby requiring less performance from the weight-bearing steel in the fire zone. This must certainly have saved lives. The external columns held. But by 10:28 their integrity was not enough. In this design of a tube within a tube, both tubes had to stand for either to survive. The North Tower core was aligned on an east-west axis, and it had been severely damaged—probably along its full length—by the airplane's centered impact. After nearly two hours of progressive weakening by fire, the remaining columns reached their limits. There was no sign of this on the outside. The South Tower of course had already fallen, and smoke was rising from a wound near the North Tower's top. Nonetheless the building remained a monolith, seemingly as permanent and strong as stone. But then the 351-foot transmission tower on the roof sank a little. The movement was barely perceptible. Half a second later the floors above the impact zone dropped as a unit straight down through the office fire, creating a flare-up and the illusion of a secondary explosion before striking the first blow in the chain of blows that pancaked the monolith to the ground . . .

Emotions were raw. One of the unacknowledged aspects of the tragedy was the jealous sense of ownership that it brought about—an unexpected but widespread feeling of something like

pride, that "this is our disaster more than yours." The feeling
started at large in the United States, and became more acute
with proximity to the site—a progression of escalating posses-
siveness that ran from the halls of Washington through subur-
ban New Jersey to New York, and from there through Lower
Manhattan to the pile itself, where it divided the three main
groups (fire, police, and construction) and sometimes set them
against one another. The firemen in particular felt that they had
a special relationship with the site, not only because they had
lost 343 people there—out of a force of 14,000—but also
because afterward their survivors, along with their dead, had
been idolized as national heroes, and subjected to the full force
of modern publicity. A few of them reacted embarrassingly, by
grandstanding on television and at public events, striking tragic
poses and playing themselves up. Even at the site, where people
generally disliked such behavior, you could find firemen signing
autographs at the perimeter gates or, after the public viewing
stand was built, drifting over to work the crowds. Most of them
behaved more soberly, no matter what pride they may secretly
have felt, if for no other reason than that their firehouse culture
had until now frowned on self-aggrandizement. Still, there was
resentment by the police, who had lost plenty of their own
people, and by the construction crews, who took it upon themselves to remember the far greater number of civilian deaths.
These tensions flared especially over the differing treatment of
human remains—on the one extreme, the elaborate flag-draped
ceremonials that the firemen accorded their own dead, and on
the other, the jaded "bag 'em and tag 'em" approach that they

took to civilians. A strange blindness caused them to persist with this behavior despite the ease with which it could have been remedied. Even Sam Melisi [a New York City firefighter] participated in it, for instance once bemoaning a "drought" to me when the remains being uncovered were merely those of civilians. It was a surprisingly ganglike view, and it encouraged a gang mentality among others on the pile . . .

And then, of course, there was the pile, always the pile. It had been the focus of ferocious energy during the collapse, and now again was the focus during the unbuilding. The pile was an extreme in itself. It was not just the ruins of seven big buildings but a terrain of tangled steel on an unimaginable scale, with mountainous slopes breathing smoke and flame, roamed by diesel dinosaurs and filled with the human dead. The pile heaved and groaned and constantly changed, and was capable at any moment of killing again. People did not merely work to clear it out but went there day and night to fling themselves against it. The pile was the enemy, the objective, the obsession, the hard-won ground . . .

The stars of the show were the machines themselves, and particularly the big diesel excavators, marvels of hydraulics and steel, which roamed through the smoke and debris on caterpillar tracks and in the hands of their operators became living things, the insatiable king dinosaurs in a world of ruin. They came in various sizes, from the "small" 320s (which could pull apart an ordinary house in minutes) to the oversized 1200s, monstrous mining machines rarely seen in New York, which proved to be too awkward for many uses on the pile. Most of the work was done by the

750s—sufficiently big, sufficiently lean, enormously persistent beasts that battled the debris without rest. Each 750 weighed in at 180,000 pounds (as compared with 140,000 pounds for the heaviest trucks, fully loaded), and was equipped with an articulating arm and one of three hydraulically powered attachments—steel-cutting "shears" (often attached to an extra-long arm, for reaching high or wreaking havoc deep inside the standing ruins); conventional "buckets," useful at the lower levels of the pile in areas of pulverized debris; or, most often, "grapplers," gap-toothed claws that could open eight feet wide, but could also close into an overbite so tight that it could snap twigs. The grappler-equipped excavators (known simply as grapplers themselves) dominated the battle until it moved well below ground. Working fast and in tandem, the machines picked the ruins apart one piece at a time. The steel they took on included the heaviest ever used in a building—box columns weighing 3,100 pounds per foot, so that a merely man-size length would amount to almost 19,000 pounds, and a fifty-foot section would come in at nearly the weight of the grappler itself. Some of the loose steel could be "flown" out by the enormous cranes that ringed the pile—but the process was so tedious that it was reserved for special cases: for instance, for lifting beams during the search for survivors among ruins too rough to allow the grapplers access, or for the dismantling of the skeletal walls, most of which were torched apart one section at a time by ironworkers in suspended baskets, and then lowered gently to the ground. This left the bulk of the fight to the grapplers, which were just tough enough to take it on.

Actually, of course, it was the operators who accepted the fight. They were said to be the best in the business, and this was easy to believe. At the start of a shift they didn't just climb aboard and sit down but seemed, rather, to strap on the equipment much as good pilots strap on their wings. Like those pilots, too, they were artists of motion—fluid, expressive, and intuitively at one with their machines. The cabs that they sat in were enclosed in wire mesh and sound-dampening, shatterproof glass; they had single comfortable seats, filtered and cooled or heated air, automotive stereos, and a combination of pedals and tightly coupled, variable-rate joysticks that allowed the operators nearly bionic control. It was the control especially that gave the grapplers their beauty. The operators might drive to work like ordinary commuters, frustrated by traffic, by parking regulations, by lines at Starbucks for insipid coffee; but after they settled into their machines, they could put all that aside, and go rumbling off into the faraway land of ruin; and if they came to terrain too wild to cross, often they could build a way through; and when they came to the field of battle, typically among other grapplers straining there, they could reach their own arms out twenty feet, clamp their own steel claws around multi-ton splinters, and with fire and smoke erupting, while shuddering and rocking forward onto the toes of their tracks, they could wrestle those splinters clear. They could also then stretch their claws wide and angle them up to use just the bottom fingers to gently stir loosened debris for the firemen to see. The operators had all that power and grace at their command, and they possessed more imagination than ordinary construction jobs had let them exercise before. Now they had been given a high purpose, and been told roughly what Sam Melisi had been told: just go and see what you can do. It was a liberation, because they knew they could do a lot. They were resourceful. They were like pioneers.

Taking risks was a necessary part of the deal. That was true for others there too: even when they were not breathing in the smoke and dust, or climbing across treacherous slopes, the workers worked on top of weakened, partially collapsed structures, which bounced and shook underfoot, and sometimes gave way. But the grappler operators were particularly exposed, not only because they led the effort, often balanced precariously and pulling on unstable debris, but also because they seemed to feel protected by the mass of their machines. This was an error. The grapplers were like dinosaurs, but with thin skins. On two occasions when they ventured into areas from which Peter Rinaldi had excluded them, the pile suddenly collapsed, dropping them into voids. The two machines were badly damaged. It was a matter purely of luck that neither of the operators was injured. Rinaldi told me he would be very surprised if no one got killed at the site. On another occasion I was with him when he noticed to his alarm that one of Tully's 750s had nosed into a corner of the partially collapsed Building Five, and was reaching up and pulling heavy debris down from overhead: Even if the building itself did not let loose, the pieces that were falling could have sliced right through the cab. Rinaldi got on the radio, which didn't work. We walked across the pile to find Jan Szumanski [superintendent of the effort to rebuild the subway line destroyed at Ground Zero]. After a period of anxiety and confusion the grappler retreated . . .

In the end, 1.5 million tons of ruins were extracted from the seventeen acres of the Trade Center site. The vast bulk of the material was barged twenty-six miles to the Fresh Kills landfill for sorting, final inspection, and burial. Despite the negative emotions it evoked in Manhattan, Fresh Kills was an excellent choice for the work—one of the largest open spaces in New York City, a magnificently barren landscape of earth-capped refuse, spreading across 2,200 acres and rising in places about 200 feet above the tidal estuaries of Staten Island. It had been retired from service six months before, in March of 2001, presumably to become a park someday, but had become reactivated for this one final purpose. Now again it was a dump, and one of the largest in the world. But it offered complete privacy and calm, and allowed for a surprising dignity during the sad and gritty operation to come . . .

"The Pentagon's Strangely Festive Ceremony"
By David Plotz
From Slate.com
September 11, 2002

Since the attacks on September 11, 2001, the huge number of dead at the World Trade Center and the heroic efforts of the United Flight 93 passengers have largely overshadowed the attacks that occurred that same day at the Pentagon. There are

many possible reasons for this. The attacks on the Pentagon
inflicted far less physical damage to the building and resulted
in far fewer casualties. Furthermore, the Pentagon houses the
Department of Defense, the military branch of the government.
Because of its sensitive operations, it must maintain a code of
secrecy. David Plotz, a Washington, D.C.–area journalist, cov-
ered the attack on the Pentagon, as well as the ceremony held
there on the first anniversary of September 11. In this piece,
Plotz tries to understand and explain why the Pentagon victims
have received so little attention compared to the other victims
of September 11.

———□———

The Pentagon 9/11 ceremony this morning feels less like a
memorial than a celebration. At the World Trade Center,
they're reading out the names of all 2,800 dead. In
Shanksville, Penn., they're tolling a bell for each Flight 93
victim. But here they run a slide show of workers rebuilding
the Pentagon, capped by a triumphal shot of a hard hat snapping together an office cubicle. The crowd of 12,000 cheers.

What is missing today? The dead. The absence of mourning is disorienting. The Pentagon's victims seem an afterthought, listed in small type in the program, and only briefly
invoked by President Bush and Secretary of Defense Donald
Rumsfeld in their speeches. For most of the hour-long ceremony,
9/11 hardly seems to matter at all. Instead, it is really a tribute
to the Phoenix Project, the massive effort that erased the damage from Flight 77 and rebuilt the Pentagon better-than-new in
less than a year.

The motto of the Phoenix Project was Todd Beamer's phrase "Let's roll." A huge sign over the dais reads "Let's roll." Thousands of Phoenix Project workers in attendance wear hard hats emblazoned with "Let's roll" stickers. Even the Navy Chaplain urges, "Let us roll" in his benediction. Today, in short, is all about rolling, about moving forward and rebuilding and winning the war, which leaves little energy to recall the grimness and despair of that day. Even on this anniversary, the Pentagon has better things to do than mourn.

Joint Chiefs of Staff Chairman Gen. Richard Myers wins the biggest cheer of the morning when he hails "the hard-hat patriots of the Phoenix Project." The hard-hat patriots in my section of the bleachers could hardly be less solemn. Their good cheer is eerie. A few seats down, a woman in a denim vest decorated with red, white, and blue stars leads a few friends in the Wave, then urges everyone to start "happy dancing." The man behind me, who owns the company that supplied the 4,900 tons of reinforced steel needed for reconstruction, has brought his wife and three sons to the festivities. He and the man in front of me, a Phoenix Project vet (whose hard hat sports Tiger Woods' autograph!), get giddy when Lee Evey walks by. Evey, the reconstruction project manager, is a rock star today. My neighbor lines up to have a photo taken with Evey. Other folks ask him for his autograph.

For months I've been trying to understand why the Pentagon attack has been a footnote to the World Trade Center and even Flight 93. Of course the scale of death and destruction at the Twin Towers dwarfed the Pentagon's loss, and of course Flight 93 offers an inspiring story of resistance. But still, the Pentagon is the pre-eminent symbol of American power, and the assault murdered nearly 200 people. You'd think it would rate more than an aside. At this morning's ceremony, I think I finally get why it doesn't.

The Pentagon event feels like someone else's family reunion. In New York, victims' family members, journalists, and politicians have done everything they could to make the Twin Towers a national tragedy, not simply a local one. They have actively sought to share their sorrow with the nation, and Americans have welcomed that. Flight 93, too, has become a national epic.

But the Pentagon is a culture of privacy (and secrecy). It didn't want public mourning. It didn't welcome the public to today's ceremony: This was "Pentagon family" only, with soldiers barring the uninvited. The Pentagon is its own world, and outsiders are outsiders. Though I've never lived in New York, I have been to the World Trade Center half-a-dozen times. I have lived in Washington for 32 years, but I had never been to the Pentagon till I picked up my press badge yesterday. The building exists for its corps of workers—tens of thousands of them—but it intentionally ignores everyone else. National security requires that; the proud, wary military culture ensures that.

The Twin Towers soared over Manhattan, visible to all. But the Pentagon is the most invisible large building you've ever seen. The building is isolated, standing in acres of parking lots. You would never stumble across it, never accidentally visit it. The Pentagon repels visitors. Barriers, Hummers, wire fences, soldiers with machine guns surround it. When I jaywalked in a Pentagon parking lot yesterday, a corporal gunned his Hummer toward me, side arm at the ready, and ordered me back to the sidewalk.

The Pentagon is far from Washington physically. The smoke and debris from the World Trade Center choked all of Lower Manhattan. The cloud from the Pentagon fire blotched one small corner of the Washington sky.

And it is far from Washington psychologically. The military is suspicious of the dominant cultures of downtown—politics, law, journalism—and the feeling is mutual. Journalists, who have had so much access to the World Trade Center, haven't breached the Pentagon. Why didn't the *Washington Post* turn the Pentagon into a crusade, as the *New York Times* did the World Trade Center? Perhaps because the *Post* and the Pentagon lived in different worlds, worlds that scarcely ever touched.

That "Pentagon family" doesn't share its sorrows. That's not military style. New York is an open, confessional, emotional city. The Pentagon is the opposite. Soldiers don't dwell on their losses in public—their lives and their work would be impossible if they did. There are too many losses.

New York has an open wound in Lower Manhattan. But the Pentagon would not show that weakness, certainly would not commemorate it a year later. This is a building that symbolizes American victory, so victory it must show. No scar remains. They rebuilt the structure perfectly, as though 9/11 never happened. Speaker after speaker today says we are not forgetting, but the building belies that. The building—with its new, clean, blank walls—has already forgotten, or rather, the building is too busy to remember. Behind those walls, they are rolling.

"Home Is Here"
By Mark Singer
From The New Yorker
October 15, 2001

The September 11 attacks were perpetrated by Al Qaeda terrorists who were Islamic radicals and mostly Arab. Most of the hijackers were from Saudi Arabia (as is Al Qaeda leader Osama bin Laden). After the attacks, a wave of anti-Arab sentiment was directed at immigrants who were either Muslim or perceived to be Muslim by some enraged and prejudiced Americans. The world's second largest Arab enclave outside of the Middle East is located in Dearborn, Michigan. Mark Singer, a staff writer for The New Yorker, *traveled to this immigrant enclave to find out how the Arab-American community felt about the September 11 attacks and how they have been treated by their neighbors since that day. What he found was that these hard-working people have faced much prejudice and discrimination. Physical violence against Arab Americans has been rare, but the attitudes toward them have often been very hostile.*

——□——

Dearborn, Michigan

In the summer of 1988, a young Arab-Israeli woman named Maha Mahajneh visited the United States at the invitation of an organization of Palestinian-American women who were holding a convention in New Jersey. It was Mahajneh's first trip to America. At the convention, she gave a talk whose topic was, indirectly, the story of her life: the challenges confronted by Arab citizens of Israel. Mahajneh happened to be an anomalous specimen of upward mobility. Growing up in Umm al-Fahm, a small city in the Galilee, she had longed for three things, at least two of which were out of the question: "I wished I was Jewish, I wished I was a man, and I wished I was rich." Clearly, however, she possessed ample self-confidence and self-awareness. Her family was Sunni Muslim, but far from devout. At eighteen, she left home. By twenty-four, she had a university degree, had settled into a cosmopolitan life in Tel Aviv, and had become the first Palestinian woman certified public accountant in Israel.

Mahajneh went on to deliver the same lecture in Chicago and Detroit, where one member of the audience was Roy Freij, a businessman whose Arabic given name is Raed. At the time of the Six-Day War, in 1967, he had been three years old and living in Jerusalem. In its aftermath, his parents decided to follow a well-travelled path to southeastern Michigan, where two hundred and fifty thousand Arabs now reside—other than Paris, the largest concentration outside the Middle East. Months of letter-writing followed Maha and Roy's first encounter, and in the spring of 1989 he flew to Israel and asked her to marry him. Within three weeks, they had wed and Maha had obtained a visa. "I wasn't thinking to come to America at all," she told me. "I came for a man I loved." In 1992, she became a United States citizen.

Maha is the chief financial officer of ACCESS, an Arab social-service and advocacy organization that operates out of eight locations in Dearborn, Michigan, offering, among other things, medical care, psychological counselling, job training and placement, adult education, and after-school programs. Dearborn has a population of a hundred thousand, more than a quarter of which is Arab; in the public schools, the figure is about fifty-eight percent. For its clients—Lebanese, Syrians, Iraqis, Palestinians, Yemenis, Jordanians, Egyptians, and North Africans—ACCESS, with a comparatively modest annual budget of ten million dollars, is a more vital presence in the community than the Ford Motor Company. Maha's office is in ACCESS's main facility, a converted school building in Dearborn's south end, a dingy district along the perimeter of Ford's gargantuan River Rouge plant.

On the morning of September 11th, she awoke at six o'clock and took a two-mile walk in Livonia, the affluent suburb west of Detroit where she lives with her husband and their two young sons. She had dropped the boys at school and was driving to the office while listening to National Public Radio when she heard the first news bulletin about the World Trade Center. Soon after she reached her desk, Maha knew that, while no work would get done that day, she and her colleagues, for symbolic and practical reasons, had to keep the doors open at all of ACCESS's facilities. Except for a three-hour bomb-scare evacuation of one building and a four-day suspension of the after-school program, they succeeded.

The names of Maha and other ACCESS executives are listed on the organization's Web site, and two days after the attack she received an E-mail from a man who attached an inflammatory newspaper column, written by Nolan Finley, an editor at the *Detroit News*, which had appeared in that morning's paper. The "least [Arab and Muslim Americans] can do for their neighbors," Finley insisted, would be to "help in every way possible to smash the network within their own communities that provides money and shelter to terrorists." In other words, what the United States government's intelligence-gathering and law-enforcement apparatus had failed to accomplish before September 11th (or since), the law-abiding Arab citizens of Detroit, in a vigilante spirit that would validate their patriotism, should undertake themselves. The E-mail sender appended his own opinion: "Talk is cheap! If you really love America, turn over the terrorist sympathizers in your midst."

Intemperately, Maha responded in kind: "Your thinking is cheap. It seems to me that you have an IQ of 10???"

In his next message, her pen pal took off the gloves: "Your remark makes it clear you support the vermin that murdered thousands of innocent Americans in New York. . . I will forward your response to the *Detroit News* and the local FBI. Terrorist scum like you have no right to be in our country."

"I'm the one who's going to forward your stupid remarks to the FBI," Maha replied. "As far as the *News*, I will not be surprised if they have more space for racist remarks from people like you. The way they did from racists like Nolan Finley."

When I paid her a visit, a week later, she seemed burdened by deepening preoccupations.

"The main thing I'm thinking now," she said, "is, after September 11th, how is it going to be for my kids? They were born in this country, and they are totally like other kids. I want my kids to be the President of the United States. Or one will be President. The other will be the adviser. I really want to believe that. At home, the day of the attack, my husband and I sat down with our sons and told them that a bad thing happened and that there might be Arabic people who caused this. We said, 'If someone at school bothers you, you answer back that these people are not representative of the Arab community. You say, "We are Americans, so don't be small-minded and include us in this."' And I keep thinking about the possible retaliation our government might take and the consequences. All our work and accomplishments—are they shattered by what happened in New York? Because we look a certain way? We are not even allowed to grieve like everyone else. People look at us like we are the enemy. I want to say, 'No, I didn't do it. I was on my way to work.' It's like Palestinians living in Israel. They're always under suspicion. And I feel that our situation here might become the same way. And if that happens where do we go? There is no place."

As narratives of immigrant journeys go, Maha's, because it is a love story, seems paradigmatic, even though it is driven neither by economic nor by political urgency. The willingness to uproot oneself and come to America and partake of what it has to offer expresses—more than any appetite for material comfort—a passion for possibility. There has always been a dark side to this evergreen tale, a shadow of dread, a xenophobia rooted not so much in fear of assault from outside aggressors as in a dull-witted suspicion of those among us who look or sound or somehow seem as if they "don't come from around here." Now that the United States actually has been assaulted from the outside, the license to feel suspicious of certain of one's neighbors has been sanctioned as an unfortunate price that the country, at war with an indiscernible foreign enemy, is willing to pay.

The migration of Arabs to Detroit in measurable numbers began in the early twentieth century. The first wave of immigrants were mostly Christians from Syria and what is now Lebanon. Muslims, attracted by job opportunities in the automobile industry, started appearing not long thereafter, and since the nineteen-sixties they have predominated, arriving in ripples that emanate from cataclysms in the Middle East—an influx of Palestinians after 1967, followed by Lebanese refugees during the late seventies and early eighties, and Iraqi Shiites in the early nineties. Nothing about the local scenery reminded the earliest arrivals of home, but today certain run-down pockets of southeast Dearborn look as if they might have been grafted on from the West Bank, and in the middle-class neighborhoods there are long commercial stretches with store signs in both Arabic and English. An average of five thousand new Arab immigrants make Detroit their port of entry each year.

In Dearborn, as in New York City, September 11th was a mayoral primary-election day. Unlike New York, Dearborn kept its polls open. The incumbent, Michael Guido, was seeking a fifth term, and although he received sixty per cent of the vote, the rules mandate a November runoff against the second-place finisher, Abed Hammoud, a thirty-five-year-old assistant prosecutor, who got eighteen per cent. Hammoud, who is Lebanese, immigrated to the United States in 1990, and likes to say that he landed in America "three days after Saddam moved into Kuwait." This dash of rhetorical color won't hurt with the Iraqi refugee vote, but he would pick that up anyway. Not that it will be enough. No one, with the possible exception of Hammoud himself, expects him to win.

For a small-city mayor, Guido, a stocky fellow in his mid-forties who favors pin-striped suits, suspenders, and monogrammed shirts with French cuffs, has been quite adept at cultivating an old-school big-city mayoral persona. During his first campaign, in 1985, he circulated a blunt-talking pamphlet that referred to Dearborn's "Arab Problem," in which he disparaged bilingual classes for Arab children in the public schools, "new neighbors [who] neglect their property," and the "'gimme, gimme, gimme' attitude" of "the so-called leadership" of the Arab community. Some Dearborn Arabs with long memories place Guido on a continuum that extends back to the heyday of Orville Hubbard, an unapologetic segregationist who was mayor from 1942 to 1977. (Hubbard is most often remembered for promoting the unsubtle motto "Keep Dearborn Clean" and for his role during the 1967 race riots in Detroit, when he took to the street to prohibit blacks from crossing into his city.) Guido has sufficient finesse to have befriended many members of the older Lebanese business establishment. But no one would accuse him of being overly solicitous toward the larger Arab population, and they are grossly underrepresented in the municipal workforce—about two and a half per cent.

Dearborn is arguably the most likely city in America where a mayoral candidate, after outlining his position on street-light maintenance, might be tossed questions about national security and would be expected to answer. Guido knows that most voters aren't all that concerned with local politics at the moment and that the less he says the better. The terrorist attack, he said, "clouds what you can do to separate yourself from your opponent." He continued, "You don't point out that your opponent is Arab-American. You talk about what you can do. What I've done for my city, I blow this guy out of the water—that should be the contest. But, you know, I have people saying, 'I'm voting for you because I don't want to vote for an Arab.' Three people have told me that in the last week. Three people telling you that out loud is like getting ten letters. And the politician's rule of thumb is that ten letters means a thousand people are thinking about it."

Or, as Hammoud said to me the week after the attack, "You think I can go knock on doors now? It's not a good time to campaign."

In the spring of 1991, after participating in uprisings against the government of Saddam Hussein, Abu Muslim al-Hayder, a Shiite college professor of computer-control engineering who was then in his mid-thirties, fled Iraq with his wife and four children. They had not been long inside a Saudi Arabian refugee camp when it became evident that it was hardly a refuge. The camp population was infested with spies for the Saddam regime and "the Saudis don't look at us as full human beings—they look at us as prisoners." After the family spent a year and a half in detention, a relief agency called the Church World Service resettled them in Washington State. There al-Hayder went back to school and subsequently tried and failed to find a job in the computer industry. Confident that his bilingual abilities made him employable, in 1995 he moved the family to Detroit.

On September 11th, al-Hayder, who has been a citizen for five years, happened to be one of the federal observers dispatched to monitor the municipal election in the town of Hamtramck, ten miles northeast of Dearborn, where there had been discrimination against Arab voters in the past. He was supposed to spend that night in a hotel and file a report the next morning, but he was allowed to leave at 9 P.M. and return to his wife and (now six) children, in Detroit.

"I found all my family scared, afraid that somebody would attack the house," he told me. Most of his neighbors had American flags displayed on their porches, and when he went to a flag store the next day it was sold out. As a short-term approach to making his allegiance plain, he tied an American-flag balloon to his balcony.

Before September 11th, al-Hayder said, he felt happy and secure. He was delighted with his children's progress in school and, in his work as ACCESS' professional liaison to the Iraqi community, he was gratified by the chance to help his newly arrived countrymen. He counts himself far more fortunate than many other erstwhile Iraqi professionals—the college teacher who now delivers pizzas; the widely published literary critic who, having failed at carpentry, is now on welfare. But he is also greatly disturbed by the American media's depiction of Muslims, most of all because of how it might affect his children's perception of themselves.

Al-Hayder has a long familiarity with, and an exceptional equanimity in the face of, the consequences of dissent. In 1978, he was imprisoned by Saddam's predecessor, Ahmad Hassan al-Bakr, and sentenced to death for his political associations, then released a year and a half later when Saddam came to power and issued an amnesty for most political prisoners. Al-Hayder remembers regarding the gesture with skepticism. "I didn't trust Saddam," he said, "because I knew that even if he gives you something he will take a lot of things more valuable."

If he saved your life, I asked, how could he take from you something more valuable?

"There are many things more valuable than your life. There is your dignity, your respect. If you live a life with no respect, it's better to die. And this is why I agreed to come to America as a refugee—better than to stay in Saudi Arabia or go to another country. But this crisis we are in is making many people, especially the media, turn away from the values that I know. If someone comes and tries to insult me for no reason, I cannot tell him thank you. A lot of people now who are colored and are American citizens, and who have a right to have weapons, may go and get a license to have weapons to defend themselves. I may even lose faith in law-enforcement agencies because they target people who are Arab and Muslims. And this is very disturbing. None of this is why I came here. I came here to be a respected human being."

On a rainy afternoon eight days after the attack, I went to the New Yasmeen Bakery, a popular establishment in north Dearborn, where John Dingell, the Democratic congressman who has represented Detroit's Downriver suburbs for forty-six years, was meeting with more than twenty Arab community leaders, mostly Lebanese businessmen and professionals. The group gathered around a square of tables in a brightly lit room and listened as Dingell praised Dearborn's Arab and non-Arab populations, noting with relief that the city had avoided the bloody spasms of anti-Arab violence (or mistaken-identity violence, as in the case of a murdered turban-wearing Sikh) that had erupted elsewhere. A couple of law-enforcement people attended, Mayor Guido sent a representative, and a tone of mutual good will prevailed. "I can't think of a single criticism of what you've done and I can't think of a single thing you haven't done that you should have," Dingell said. "This community has made me proud. You have shown yourselves to be exemplary Americans, and I apologize to you for any of the hurts that have been inflicted upon you." That was the good news. The ominous downside was implicit in several questions posed to Dingell: What about government proposals to expand wiretapping authority? What about the ratcheting up of racial profiling and the broadened application of "secret evidence" (the tactic authorities use to detain immigrants without explanation)? Abed Hammoud cited a fresh Gallup poll which showed that fifty-eight per cent of Americans favored requiring Arabs, United States citizens included, to go through "special, more intensive" security screenings at airports.

Dingell didn't gloss over any of these concerns. "I can tell you," he said, "that the events of last Tuesday are not going to be useful to us in terms of protecting basic liberties."

Inauspicious in a different way were snatches of conversation I overheard before the meeting got under way—a sifting through rumors that reflected the awfulness of feeling marginalized, a grasping at anything remotely self-exculpatory. Hadn't there been news reports that some of the alleged terrorist pilots had turned up alive in Saudi Arabia? (And if they hadn't been flying the planes, who had? Europeans, perhaps?) For days, an E-mail had circulated concerning the newsreel footage, first shown on CNN, of Palestinians celebrating in East Jerusalem in the hours after the attack; it was ten-year-old videotape, several people assured me, recycled from the Gulf War, when Iraqi missiles landed in Israel. (After I returned to New York, I checked CNN's Web site, where conclusive evidence was posted that the claim of hoax was a hoax.)

The next day, I dropped by the office of the *Arab American News* and met with the editor, the inconveniently named Osama Siblani, who'd been collecting factoids as well as incendiary phone messages, some of which he played for me. Many were bizarrely disgusting (e.g., the rant from a fellow whose favorite television programs were being preempted by the prime-time news blanket: he wanted Arab corpses fed to the sharks in Florida), but most were just plain chilling. Siblani also expressed dismay at the half-dozen E-mails he'd received urging him to publish the "fact" that four thousand Jews had mysteriously not shown up for work at the World Trade Center on September 11th. Was Dearborn a place where, unavoidably, two startlingly divergent realities had taken root? Or was the nuttiness symptomatic of a profound urge to insulate oneself from reality altogether? More than once, I heard Arabs express the fear that a "Dearborn connection" to terrorism might materialize.

Alas—the law of percentages dictated as much—that had already occurred. The day of the gathering at the New Yasmeen Bakery, a screamer headline in the *Detroit Free Press* said "TERRORIST TASK FORCE ARRESTS 3 IN DETROIT." Federal agents looking for Nabil al-Marabh, a presumed associate of Osama bin Laden, had raided an apartment on the southwest side, just outside Dearborn. Al-Marabh wasn't present (he was captured later in the week, near Chicago), but the three men who were arrested reportedly had false identification papers as well as a notebook that made reference in Arabic to an American base in Turkey. As the story unfolded over the next few days, it emerged that last year, in Dearborn, al-Marabh obtained licenses to drive large trucks with hazardous cargoes. Two of the other suspects, Ahmed Hannan and Karim Koubriti, attended a commercial truck-driving school this past summer.

Their tuition of thirty-three hundred dollars apiece had been paid by ACCESS, a revelation that obviously pained Ismael Ahmed, the executive director. "We send people to all kinds of training programs and we don't check their political credentials," he told the *Free Press*. "All they have to do is come here looking for a job." In fact, Ahmed told me, he is working with the authorities. "There's a legitimate investigation of terrorism, and we think people should be cooperating," he said. "But we're not telling our community to march into the ovens. I just read a survey that shows sixty-one per cent of Arab-Americans agree that profiling is justified. That's a symptom of plain fear. That's not what they truly believe, but when they're asked about this in the context of national security, that's what they're going to say."

Ahmed Mohamed Esa is a short, slightly built, soft-voiced forty-eight-year-old man with a cropped white beard, black hair, a gap between his front teeth, and thick dark rings beneath his eyes. Since 1976, he has divided his life between Yemen and Dearborn, where he shares with two other Yemenis a five-hundred-dollar-a-month three-room flat. In Yemen, Esa has a wife and six sons. They live three hours from the city of Taiz, in Makbana, a village with no telephone and no electricity. None of them have ever seen America. Until the day after the attack on the World Trade Center, Esa had worked at a small welding company for fifteen years—longer than everyone except the company's owner, Paul Rakoczy. He earned $12.36 an hour and usually put in an eight-and-a-half-hour day. Whatever money he saved he sent to his wife, unless he was bringing it in person; each year, he spends at least three or four months with his family.

On September 12th, Esa told me, he arrived at the welding shop at 5:40 A.M.—around the time the muezzin at his neighborhood mosque was uttering the morning prayer call—and punched the clock. Then: "I go take my work uniform. When I hear the whistle for the work, I take my coffee and go to take my gloves and go to see Mr. Paul what I work on today. He say complete the job from yesterday. I start to work. I'm working twenty minutes, a half hour, and he say to me, 'Don't work. Go home.' I tell him, 'Why I go home?' He say, 'You are Arabic, you are Muslim. You don't see what happened in New York, in Washington? You don't see how many people your people killed?' I tell him I not do nothing. I work here. I have been here fifteen years. How I can go home? He say, 'I can see your face. Go pray in your mosque. Go pray with your leader. I don't want you to work here.' For a half minute or a minute, I thinking what I can do. He say, 'If you don't go, I get the police for you.' I hear that, I say maybe there is trouble, so I go. I have my check coming the next day, but I don't go get it. I'm too scared. I think maybe if I go there he do something, I don't know."

After finding his way to an ACCESS counselling center, Esa told his story to me and to a reporter for the *Free Press*, who in turn tracked down Rakoczy. Though Rakoczy disputed elements of Esa's account—he had not fired him outright but had told him to take the rest of the week off—he made no attempt to conceal his feelings about Islam. "As far as I'm concerned, their religion is done," he said. "When these guys ran their plane in there like that and hurt all those people, that was the end of it right there. That made their religion—you might as well write it as I say it—the scum of the earth." (Last week, a lawyer for Esa filed a discrimination suit against Rakoczy.)

I asked Esa whether his wife knew that the family no longer had an income.

"I speak to her sometimes once a week, sometimes once a month," he said. "If she come to the city, she will call. She doesn't know what happened with my job. She maybe doesn't know what happened in New York. I maybe will talk to her today. Maybe tomorrow."

When I asked whether he had plans to look for another job, he smiled, shrugged, and said, "How can I face an American guy and ask him to work? How can I knock the door and say I'm an Arabic guy? He might kill me."

So what was he planning to do next?

He smiled and shrugged again.

"America has changed like the weather. You not see America how is it? I sleep on Monday. I get up in the morning on Tuesday. Now I don't know what tomorrow will happen. Tomorrow. I don't know. Tomorrow is too far."

CHAPTER THREE

INDIVIDUAL DEVELOPMENT AND IDENTITY: THE MAKING OF TERRORISTS AND HEROES

"A Nation Challenged: The Mastermind; A Portrait of the Terrorist: From Shy Child to Single-Minded Killer"
By Jim Yardley with reporting by Neil MacFarquhar and Paul Zielbauer
From the New York Times
October 10, 2001

The motivation of Islamic terrorists is something that is hotly debated. It is often contended that terrorists are simply unthinking actors, puppets whose strings are pulled by some madman who always himself remains out of harm's way. Others feel that no matter how misguided they are, terrorists passionately believe in a cause for which they will risk imprisonment, torture, and even death. Insight into the disputed motives and character of terrorists can often be gained by examining the life stories of these men and the events that led up to their entry into a terrorist group. Mohamed Atta, the leader of the September 11 Al Qaeda cells, was born in Egypt and grew up under its repressive government and crippled economy. While in Egypt, he had

*shown no tendency toward the religious extremism that
ultimately came to define his life. So what drove a man who had
finally escaped the harsh Egyptian life to reject and attack the
Western world that had offered him opportunity, freedom, and
safe haven? In this profile,* New York Times *correspondents Jim
Yardley, Neil MacFarquhar, and Paul Zielbauer attempt to
answer these questions by revealing Atta's personal history.*

———□———

Mr. Atta's path to Sept. 11, pieced together from interviews with
people who knew him across 33 years and three continents, was
a quiet and methodical evolution of resentment that somehow—
and that how remains the essential imponderable—took a leap
to mass-murderous fury.

The youngest child of a pampering mother and an ambi-
tious father, Mr. Atta was a polite, shy boy who came of age in
an Egypt torn between growing Western influence and the religious fundamentalism that gathered force in reaction. But it
was not until he was on his own, in the West, that his religious
faith deepened and his resentments hardened. The focus of his
disappointment became the Egyptian government; the target of
his blame became the West, and especially America . . .

A Shy and Sheltered Boy

The genteel gloss of the Abdein neighborhood of Cairo had
dulled to shabby disrepair by the early 1980's when Mohamed
al-Amir Atta entered his teenage years. The government workers who had once lived well on $100 a month found them-
selves in a vortex of downward mobility, working second and
third jobs to survive.

Mr. Atta's father, a lawyer, considered his neighbors inferior, even if he, too, feared the economic undertow. Neighbors recalled an arrogant man who often passed without a word or a glance.

The family was viewed as thoroughly modern, the two daughters headed for careers as a professor and a doctor. The father was the disciplinarian, grumbling that his wife spoiled their bright, if timid, son, who continued to sit on her lap until enrolling at Cairo University.

"I used to tell her that she is raising him as a girl, and that I have three girls, but she never stopped pampering him," Mohamed al-Amir Atta Sr. recalled in a recent interview at his apartment.

In a high school classroom of 26 students grouped by their shared given name, Mohammed Hassan Attiya recalled that Mr. Atta focused solely on becoming an engineer—and following his father's bidding.

"I never saw him playing," Mr. Attiya said. "We did not like him very much, and I think he wanted to play with the rest of the boys, but his family, and I think his father, wanted him to always perform in school in an excellent way."

The social, political and religious pressures roiling Egypt exploded in 1981 with the assassination of President Anwar el-Sadat, the first Arab leader to make peace with Israel. Fundamentalists decried him as a puppet of the West, a traitor to Islam.

Even for a boy as sheltered as Mr. Atta, the disillusionment on the streets would have been difficult to ignore. His father, without explanation, says his son began to pray in earnest at 12 or 13, an awakening that coincided closely with Sadat's slaying. But the elder Mr. Atta said his son's religious inclination did not extend to politics.

"I advised him, like my father advised me, that politics equals hypocrisy," his father said.

The boy refused to join a basketball league because it was organized by the Muslim Brotherhood, Egypt's most established religious political organization, which also recruited from Cairo University's engineering department but not, apparently, Mr. Atta, who graduated from there in 1990.

His degree meant little in a country where thousands of college graduates were unable to find good jobs. Though Mr. Atta found work with a German company in Cairo and was reluctant to leave his mother and sisters, his father convinced him that only an advanced degree from abroad would allow him to prosper in Egypt. Soon he was headed to Hamburg Technical University on scholarship.

"I told him I needed to hear the word 'doctor' in front of his name," his father recalled. "We told him your sisters are doctors and their husbands are doctors and you are the man of the family."

From initial appearances, the slender young Mr. Atta remained the same person in Hamburg that he had been in Egypt—polite, distant and neatly dressed. He answered a classified ad and was hired part-time at an urban planning firm, Plankontor. He impressed his co-workers with his diligence and the careful elegance of his drafting.

Yet he must have felt unmoored, on his own in a strange land. He took refuge in the substantial population of Turkish, African and Arab immigrants living in the blue-collar Harburg section surrounding the university. There, his religious faith, still tentative in Egypt, took deeper hold.

He brought a prayer carpet to his job and carefully adhered to Islamic dietary restrictions, shunning alcohol and checking the ingredients of everything, even medicine. He had his choice of three mosques, but the two closest to campus were dominated by Turks, whom many local Arabs disdained as less devout and too sympathetic to America.

Instead, Mr. Atta often prayed at the Arabic-language Al-Tauhid mosque, a bleak back room of a small shop where the imam, Ahmed Emam, preached that America was an enemy of Islam and a country "unloved in our world." . . .

In November 1997 he paid an unexpected visit to his academic supervisor, Professor Machule, to discuss his thesis, then disappeared again for about a year. Federal officials say they have strong evidence that he trained at an Al Qaeda camp in Afghanistan during the late 1990s, which could explain his whereabouts in 1998.

He reappeared in Hamburg in early 1999, the period that German investigators connect him with the cell of about 20 other suspected terrorists . . . Mr. Atta's degree had been on hold; suddenly, finishing it became imperative. He submitted his thesis in August 1999. When he successfully defended his thesis, graduating with high honors, Mr. Atta refused to shake hands with one of the two judges, a woman.

His father has told reporters that his son earned a masters degree in Germany, but in fact, Mr. Atta received only an undergraduate degree. But his attentions were already elsewhere. He began preparing to go to America.

A Disciplined Perfectionist

With few exceptions, Mohamed Atta regarded the Americans who crossed his path with the same contempt his father once reserved for his Cairo neighbors. He was polite when he had to be—to rent a car or an airplane—but the mildness recalled by his friends in Egypt and Germany was gone, as was his beard.

He arrived in June at Newark International Airport and would spend the next 15 months in near perpetual motion, earning a pilot's license in Florida during the last six months of 2000, then spending the first nine months of 2001 traveling across the country and at least twice to Europe.

The awful efficiency of the attack demanded a leader with a precise and disciplined temperament, and Mr. Atta apparently filled that role. Federal investigators have told a House committee that in the fall of 2000, as he was in the middle of flight training in Venice, Fla., Mr. Atta received a wire transfer of more than $100,000 from a source in the United Arab Emirates. Investigators believe the source was Mustafa Ahmad, thought to be an alias for Shaykh Said, a finance chief for Mr. bin Laden.

For much of 2001, Mr. Atta appeared to make important contacts with other hijackers or conspirators. He traveled twice to Spain, in January and July, and officials are investigating whether he met with Al Qaeda contacts. He also used Florida as a base to move around the United States, including trips to Atlanta, where he rented a plane, to New Jersey, where he may have met with other hijackers, and at least two trips to Las Vegas. Everywhere he went, he made hundreds of cell phone calls and made a point to rent computers for e-mails, including at a Las Vegas computer store, Cyberzone, where customers can play a video game about terrorists with a voice that declares "terrorists win."

While Mr. Atta was considered a perfectionist, he was not infallible. Brad Warrick, owner of a rental agency in South Florida where Mr. Atta returned a car two days before the attack, found an ATM receipt and a white Post-it note that became key evidence. Mr. Atta's decision to wire $4,000 overseas shortly before the attacks left an electronic trail that investigators believe is leading back to Al Qaeda. Finally, authorities found his luggage at Logan Airport in Boston, containing, among other things, his will. It remains unclear if the bag simply missed the connection to his flight.

Or perhaps the introvert, the meticulous planner, the man who believed he was doing God's will, wanted to make certain the world knew his name.

Among the Heroes: United Flight 93 and the Passengers and Crew Who Fought Back
By Jere Longman
2002

Questions still remain about what exactly happened to United Flight 93 over Shanksville, Pennsylvania, on the morning of

September 11, 2001. This much is certain, however: a group of passengers bravely attempted to retake control of the plane that the terrorists had hijacked and seemed to be pointing toward the nation's capital. Every one of these passengers is a hero, including a 31-year-old man named Mark Bingham. Bingham's story is a true tragedy. His life seemed to be a study in contrasts. He was a gay rugby player and fraternity member. He grew up homeless at times and usually without money, yet he became successful nevertheless, owning his own public relations company while still in his twenties. If a person's character helps determine their destiny, Mark Bingham seemed destined to become a hero. This selection is taken from New York Times *reporter Jere Longman's* Among the Heroes, *a celebration of the heroes of Flight 93 and a recounting of their life stories.*

———□———

At six forty-four on the West Coast—nine forty-four in the East—the phone rang at Vaughn Hoglan's ranch-style home in Saratoga, California. It was the beginning of yet another busy day in the home. In the past two years, Vaughn and his wife, Kathy, had become parents to five babies by surrogate mothers. Alice Hoglan, Vaughn's sister, had delivered four of the babies herself. Just six months earlier, at age fifty-one, Alice had given birth to triplets. "Just lending out the womb," she joked. Alice was a flight attendant for United and was staying at her brother's house to help care for the kids. When the phone rang, a family friend and baby-sitter, Carol Phipps, answered in the kitchen. It was Mark Bingham, Alice's son.

"Get Kathy or Alice quickly," he said.

Carol walked down the hallway to Kathy Hoglan's room.

"There is an urgent call," Carol said. "Come quickly."

Kathy hurried out of bed and ran into the kitchen.

"Kathy, it's Mark. I'm on United Flight 93 and it's been hijacked."

Kathy Hoglan grabbed a piece of paper and wrote "United 93." Mark sounded calm, matter-of-fact.

"I wanted to call to tell you, in case I never see you again, that I love you," Mark said.

Kathy's mind raced. They'll negotiate, land the plane safely, everything will be okay. How did he make the call? Is he in danger from making the call? Mark's voice sounded as if a situation had been resolved in his mind. He sounded like a person who knew what was going to happen, or might happen, and maybe things were not going to turn out the way he would like. As if he felt he might die but that he still had hopes of making it through.

"Oh my gosh, let me get your mom for you," Kathy told Mark.

Alice Hoglan had heard her sister-in-law race down the hallway and say, "Well, we love you, too, Mark."

She got to the kitchen and Kathy told her, "Talk to Mark, he's been hijacked."

"Hi, Mark," Alice said.

There was a stiff formality in his response.

"Mom, this is Mark Bingham." . . .

On the phone now, Mark told his mother that he loved her. He kept a sign in his San Francisco office that said ALICE HOGLAN IS A GODDESS. It was not unusual for Mark to call Alice to express his love, but it was unusual for him to do it at

six forty-four in the morning. His voice sounded controlled and
rattled at the same time.

"I'm on a flight from Newark to San Francisco," Mark
said. "There are three guys aboard who say they have a bomb."

"Who are these guys, Mark?"

There was a long pause. Alice listened and listened.
Mark did not answer for what seemed like five seconds. She
heard voices, nothing suggesting violence or threats, no
yelling, no accented voices. It sounded as if someone were
speaking to him confidentially. It reminded Alice of an office
setting, the kinds of ambient noises a person heard if someone
laid the phone down for a minute, or turned away.

Then Mark came back on the line. "Do you believe me?
It's true."

He was seeking assurance.

"I do believe you, Mark," Alice said. "Who are these guys?"

There was another long pause. Alice visualized ominous things. Mark said he was calling from an Airfone. He
might be in full view of the hijackers. He was probably in
first class, she thought, and the hijackers were probably up
there. She worried that he was drawing attention to himself,
making himself a target.

A long pause followed after she asked him who these
guys were. It was as if he did not hear his mother, or someone else was speaking to him. Then the line went dead. She
worried that he had been thrown off the phone or that the
hijackers had knifed him.

By then, her brother Vaughn had turned on the television in the living room. They saw a horrific replay, one tower

of the World Trade Center in flames and the other tower being approached by what appeared to be a slow-moving airplane. It seemed surreal to Alice, like a horror movie.

At that moment, Alice understood. She felt that Mark knew what he was up against, that maybe someone had organized a plan, that he knew the situation was dire and he was calling to say good-bye in case he did not see her again.

Then news came of a third plane hitting the Pentagon. It was apparent now that Mark's plane was a piece of a larger horrible mosaic. Alice and Vaughn and Kathy thrashed about for something to do, some way to help, and Vaughn said, "Get Mark on the phone and tell him it's a suicide mission. Tell him they need to do whatever they can to try to get control back."

Alice dialed Mark's cell phone number. Later, she would retrieve the message from the phone company, one of more than forty urgent messages sent to her son.

"Hey, Mark, this is Dad," Jerry Bingham said from Florida, emotion in his voice. "I'm just calling to see how you're doing. Uh, I'm looking at that big wreck, man," a reference to the World Trade Center. "I hope you're not too close to that. So give me a call when you can," he said, his voice breaking.

Other friends called Mark's cell phone, and so did his assistant at his public relations firm, wondering whether he was flying, reminding him that she had set up a business call for him.

A friend named Ken called. "I'm in absolute shock now," he said in his message. "I can't get over what is happening. Oh my God, this is just devastating."

Then Alice called the cell phone. "Mark, this is your mom," she said. She gave the incorrect time, ten fifty-four. It was actually nine fifty-four in the East. "The news is that it's been hijacked by terrorists. They are planning to probably use the plane as a target to hit some site on the ground. If you possibly can, try to overpower these guys, 'cause they'll probably use the plane as a target."

She was nervous and she kept saying "target" instead of "missile."

"I would say, go ahead and do everything you can to overpower them, because they're hell-bent," Alice said. "Try to call me back if you can. You know the number here."

She gave two numbers.

"Okay, I love you sweetie, good-bye."

To act in the face of danger or fear would not have been out of character for Mark. He had been a sensitive, awkward kid, insecure about his physical ability until high school, when he began playing rugby. By then, he and his mother were living in the Santa Cruz Mountains south of San Francisco, in a rustic cabin whose roof once collapsed in a rainstorm. By virtue of geography, Mark attended public high school in the wealthy enclave of Los Gatos. Alice Hoglan would stand on the sideline in agony, watching her son fulfill the game's motto: Give blood, play rugby. Mark's coach could not remember another player who bled so much or got injured so often. His nose became a career's crooked resume. But with rugby, Mark's social and physical ungainliness disappeared. In motion, he was a different person, bold, ceaseless, as if awkwardness could be overcome like inertia. His friends were amazed to see him running, headlong, his huge body amped on unpadded adrenaline, craving clean, hard, disruptive contact. There were no protective helmets or shoulder pads in rugby, no plastic-and-leather shock absorbers, nothing but the grunting slap of muscle and bone, the great satisfactory jab of a shoulder into an opponent's chest, that one crystalline instant of domination, that absolute, presiding moment over failing legs and helpless exhale.

"He was like a guided missile, head down, going," said Dave Kupiecki, who attended the University of California at Berkeley with Mark and in whose wedding Mark served as best man. "He wasn't that fast, but he was everywhere. No matter how hard a guy ran into him, he kept going. I was overwhelmed. I'd never seen anyone play sports who was always moving." . . .

Emboldened by his athletic success, self-assured, his confidence having filled out along with his physique, the social outsider having become an insider in campus athletic and fraternity life, Mark made an announcement in August of 1991 that his family and friends found stunning: he was gay. He first told his mother after they spent a day together, driving home into the sunset from the East Bay. They were more brother and sister than mother and son, and they leaned on each other, talked about everything. On this day, Alice was grousing to him about a man she was dating, when Mark said, "There is something I promised myself I'd tell you before the sun went down."

She could tell by the tone in his voice that something serious was weighing on him.

"I'm gay," Mark said.

Alice was grateful that her son had told her, but astounded at the same time, and she did not remember much else of what was said.

"It's news I don't think any parent really wants to hear," Alice said. "I could tell it meant a lot to him that I would be accepting. I struggled with it. I made calls, researched it, educated myself. Essentially, I hid my chagrin from him. I was riddled with stereotypes. It was weeks, months maybe, before I was able to come to peace with it. I knew it was not a choice that he had made. I knew the last thing Mark needed was resistance or rejection from his loved ones."

He had been afraid to come out, his friends said, not because he was ashamed but because he worried that intractable beliefs might make others think less of him. Mark Wilhelm, a friend who said he met Mark Bingham in 1990, wrote that Mark had sensed since he was twelve that he was gay, and that he feared his friends and family would find out. "I'd have to kill myself," he remembered Mark saying, afraid his family would no longer love him. Mark eventually made this difficult admission while a member of two groups long known for homophobic behavior: Frat boys and jocks. His acknowledgment shook up the belief systems of many who knew him, shattered stereotypes. Mark could be defined only in the sense that he was undefinable. He was a rugby player, a frat boy, a yuppie, a Libertarian who would later help organize a fund-raiser for John McCain's Republican presidential campaign, and he was gay.

"He didn't like anyone trying to put him in a box; that drove him nuts," said Todd Sarner, a longtime friend. "He brushed aside old prejudices about what a jock or a gay person is."

And yet, so resistant was he to being stereotyped, said a friend, Bryce Eberhart, that on Mark's laundry list of personality traits being gay "was number eight or nine, behind being a decent pickup basketball player." . . .

After calling her son's cell phone, Alice Hoglan hung up. Then she called Mark again and left a second message. Her voice was hurried, pressing, but not panicked.

"Mark, apparently it's terrorists and they're hell-bent on crashing the aircraft," Alice said. "So, if you can, try to take over the aircraft. There doesn't seem to be much plan to land the aircraft normally, so I guess your best bet would be to try to take it over if you can, or tell the other passengers. There is one flight that they say is headed toward San Francisco. It might be yours. So, if you can, group some people and perhaps do the best you can to get control of it. I love you, sweetie. Good luck. Good-bye."

At her apartment in nearby San Jose, California, Candyce Hoglan had a troubling dream. She was Alice Hoglan's sister. Both were United flight attendants. She dreamed of a plane going down, of people begging for their lives, of passengers screaming, "No, no." She awoke disturbed. The dream had been so real. A few minutes later, the phone rang. It was her brother Lee Hoglan. Their nephew Mark was on a plane that had been hijacked . . .

In the end, what happened remained more murky than clear. The details had to be confirmed by the character of the passengers and crew, beyond the validation of voices on a tape or words on a transcript. Even if they didn't reach the cockpit, or reached it too late to gain control of the plane, their bravery was not diminished. It is uncertain how far they got, but it is clear they got as far as they could. They set out that morning as businessmen and businesswomen, students, vacationers eagerly leaving the congested city for open spaces, a mourning stepfather going to retrieve the remains of his stepson. In the final desperate minutes, they were all trying to get home safely to their families. Their personal courage became a wider heroism. Their accomplishment lay in the bold effort. They were scared, but they did not let fear overwhelm them. They knew the odds were slim, but they retaliated with headlong valor and prevented the terrorists from reaching their target. At a time of grieving, confused, enraged vulnerability, when the United States appeared defenseless against an unfamiliar foe, the passengers and crew of Flight 93 provided the solace of defiance. They fought back, bringing a measure of victory to unthinkable defeat.

Firehouse
By David Halberstam
2002

Since the September 11 attacks, New York City firefighters and police officers have become nationwide symbols of heroism. NYPD and FDNY action figures, T-shirts, and baseball caps began to show up everywhere, and the departments' men and women became celebrities of a sort. The two departments

*lost many of their members in the collapse of the World Trade
Center, but the FDNY was particularly devastated. Most of its
leadership was killed in the towers, and some firehouses lost
most of their firefighters. For years, firefighters and firehouses
had gone virtually unnoticed in New York. They were just
another ingredient in the daily fabric of life. Then, within a
couple of horrific hours, more than 300 firefighters perished
doing a job that the rest of the city had taken for granted for
so long. David Halberstam, a Pulitzer Prize–winning journalist
and author, took it upon himself to write the history of his
neighborhood firehouse—Engine 40, Ladder 35—and to
memorialize the twelve men from the house who died when
they ran into the burning towers to help others run out.*

———□———

Firemen live in a world apart from other civilians. The rest of
the world seems to change, but the firehouses do not. This is, in
fact, as close to a hermetically sealed world as you are likely to
find in contemporary America: It is driven by its unique needs,
norms, and traditions, some of which are inviolable. The New
York Fire Department is largely male—women have in recent
years become firefighters, but that has happened slowly, and
many houses have remained all-male, including 40/35—and
largely white, and it is to an uncommon degree composed of men
who come from firefighting families, men who, like their fathers
before them, have wanted to be firemen since childhood.

A great deal of the tradition and the coherence is family-
driven, with generation after generation supplying men to the
department. It is almost as if there is a certain DNA strand
found in firefighting families, where the men are pulled toward

the job because their fathers and uncles were firemen and had loved it, and because some of their happiest moments when they were boys had come when they visited the firehouse and these big, gruff men made a fuss over them. The job and the mission and the sense of purpose that go with it have always been quietly blended into the family fabric. "It's passed on father to son, and sometimes grandfather to father to son," says the Reverend Robert Scholz, who is the pastor of a Lutheran church located about three blocks from the 40/35 firehouse and who knows the men well. "You see your father doing it, and you're proud of him. His life seems honorable and purposeful, and you see the richness of his friendships and the loyalty of these men to each other, and how, when you're young, the other firemen seem like additional uncles. And it seems so honorable."

All of this makes the department's hold on the men quite striking in an age when the lure of material and other ego rewards is so powerful. The hold the New York Fire Department has on the young men of the city and its environs is as strong as ever. The waiting list to get into the depart-ment is long, so long that many young men who want to be firemen start as cops and transfer to the fire department when their numbers finally come up. Yet the pay is marginal. According to one department veteran, a young married fireman with four children and a wife who doesn't work makes so little that he is technically eligible for food stamps. Almost all of the men at 40/35 could double their pay in other jobs.

Terry Holden, who has been at 40/35 since 1964 and who has seen the personnel turn over more than once, says of the unusual sense of continuity: "It's completely different from when I first came here. There's not a single person left from back then. And the country and the city are very different, and yet the house in most important ways is exactly the same—even though it's a completely different generation from a very different era. It's as if we've been cloned. Part of it is that the talent pool is so similar—we come from the same places, the same kind of families, sometimes even the same parochial schools, and we have the same values. And we still have the same purpose, though we don't like to talk about it openly. But we like it when we get back to the firehouse after a fire and someone says you did a good job. Especially when you tell that to the junior men."

A firehouse, most firemen believe, is like a vast extended second family—rich, warm, joyous, and supportive, but on occasion quite edgy as well, with all the inevitable tensions brought on by so many forceful men living so closely together over so long a period of time. What gradually emerges is surprisingly nuanced; the cumulative human texture has slowly evolved over time and is often delicate. It is created out of hundreds of unseen, unknown, and often unidentified tiny adjustments that these strong, willful men make to accommodate one another, sometimes agreeably and sometimes grudgingly. It incorporates how the men live with one another day in and day out, and surprisingly the degree to which, whether they realize it or not, they come to love one another (sometimes even as they dislike one another)—because love is a critical ingredient in the fireman's code, which demands that you are willing to risk your life for your firehouse brothers.

The men not only live and eat with one another, they play sports together, go off to drink together, help repair one another's houses, and, most important, share terrifying risks; their loyalties to one another, by the demands of the dangers they face, must be instinctive and absolute. Thus are firehouse codes fashioned. When a probie—a probationary or apprentice firefighter—joins a firehouse, he must adjust to the firehouse culture, rather than the firehouse adjusting to him. It is like the military in that respect: Idiosyncrasy can come later; adherence to the rules and traditions comes first.

Reverend Scholz long ago decided that there was something special to firemen amid their traditions, that they had chosen this profession because it expanded their lives and gave those lives additional meaning. Many of the men, he said, were not necessarily angels or saintly—far from it, in fact—and they were not, in the traditional sense, necessarily very religious. But there was also a certain spiritual redemption to what they did. They could be on occasion rowdy and combative and they had their allotted share of human flaws, of which they themselves were often all too aware. But whatever they had done wrong the night before, the next morning when they were at the firehouse, they were able to take extra meaning from their lives, and to find some form of redemption because of the nature of the job, because of the risks they take for complete strangers.

Scholz believed that outsiders would never be able to understand who these men were and what they did unless they understood the job for what it is—nothing less than a calling. Jim Gormley, now captain of Engine 40, completely agreed. "We all have our daily conversation with God," Gormley once said. "Do we do what we do for God? No. But it's there, the religious part, just the same. We do it for people. We do it for the sense of rightness. And we like doing it, like the life because we're never ashamed of what we do." . . .

If any one moment brought home the sheer human horror of that day, it was when John Morello, father of Vincent Morello, one of the men from 40/35, found out what had happened. In the early-morning hours of Wednesday, September 12, John, a retired battalion chief, was still trying to determine what had happened to Vincent, who was listed as being on Ladder 35 and was missing. Communications with fire authorities had been terrible; the city's Emergency Command Center in 7 World Trade Center had been destroyed early in the terrorist attack, and any real information had been sketchy.

It had been some seventeen hours since the Ladder 35 rig left the house, and Morello, fearful of the worst, but having no inkling how bad the worst really was, had been calling various private department phone numbers he knew. He was by this time with his daughter-in-law Debi at her and Vincent's home in Middle Village, Queens. Finally, around 2:30 AM, he got through to someone. Morello explained that he was a retired battalion chief and that his son had been down at the World Trade Center. The man at the other end of the line agreed to help him. Morello did not realize that Debi was listening in on the first-floor extension. "Thirty-five Truck," the man had said. "Thirty-five Truck is missing."

"What the hell does that mean, Thirty-five Truck is missing?" Morello asked. "The whole company is missing?"

"Yes," said the man at the other end, "the whole company is missing." That was when John Morello heard Debi on the line, screaming in agony, not just for herself, it seemed, but for every family member connected to 40/35 and all the other New York firehouses that day.

September 11 was a special kind of hell for 40/35. No one who works at the firehouse has really yet comprehended the apocalyptic nature of what occurred. That morning thirteen men set out on the house's two rigs, and twelve of them died. It was a tragedy beyond comprehension, not just the worst day in the history of New York City, but one of the worst days in American history—a day that people would compare to Pearl Harbor, sixty years earlier. The New York Fire Department was the institution that bore the brunt of it—343 men killed—and the 40/35 firehouse was among the hardest hit. The aftershocks of the tragedy have persisted not just in the grief for the men who were lost, but also in the guilt among the survivors, who have continued to wonder not just why they lived, but whether it was wrong to have done so. There have been acceptable days, and there have been bad days, when the pain was almost unbearable.

The men of 40/35 are bonded now more than ever, not just by their job, as in the past, but by their grief as well. Sometimes the house has the feeling of a World War II unit, in which a good part of the men were wiped out in one sudden, shocking battle, and none of the survivors entirely under-stands what happened—why so many men were taken so cruelly and so quickly, and why they, the survivors, were spared. So much of who went that morning and who did not was chance. Some were relieved early and were on their way home before they heard about the attack; some were supposed to have worked that day but had taken what are called mutuals, which meant that, for personal reasons, they had switched shifts with other men . . .

Back at the firehouse, there was a darkening sense of what was happening, of how terrible it was, a tragedy beyond anyone's comprehension. By the early afternoon, there was talk that the department might have lost more than 300 men. Most of those gathering back at Sixty-sixth Street—many of them sent in from other houses—knew all too well from watching television and seeing both buildings pancake down that this collapse was likely to have been fatal to anyone under it. Gradually, there was a strong sense that the unthinkable had happened, that every man they had sent down from 40/35 might have died. Throughout the day, there were more and more reports, and the news was unrelentingly bad. Not only had their own men probably been lost, but also a number of other firemen with exceptionally close ties to the firehouse, men who still palled around with the 40/35 men: Larry Virgilio, who had worked there for years before going over to Squad 18 (a special unit committed to dealing with hazardous materials); Mike Boyle and David Arce, the boyhood friends who had become firemen together and, even after moving on to Engine 33, still played on the 40/35 softball team; and Larry Stack, a big strapping man of about six feet four inches who had served as a lieutenant at 40/35 in the early '80s, and had worked there as well as a covering captain when one of the house's regular officers was either sick or on vacation. Stack was widely regarded by the men as an almost perfect officer, balancing an instinctive sense of command with just the right amount of warmth, which he always seemed to summon at just the right time. Slowly it dawned on everyone that they were witnesses to, and part of, the worst day in firefighting history.

"Mayor of the World"
By Eric Pooley
From Time
December 31, 2001

> Rudolph "Rudy" Giuliani is too complex a man to simply describe or characterize. While he was a source of great strength, stability, and reassurance for shaken New Yorkers in the days following the September 11 World Trade Center attack, during the previous seven years of his mayoral tenure, he had often been extremely unpopular. Mirroring nationwide trends, New York City's crime rate dropped considerably under Giuliani. Creating a "new New York" had come at a heavy price, however. An enlarged police force and tourist-oriented redevelopment of seedy areas of town drove the city into debt. Furthermore, Giuliani did little to ease racial tensions following a string of police shootings of unarmed black men. Yet thanks to his remarkable display of courage and calm on September 11, 2001, and the days following, Giuliani is now known as the Mayor of the World. In December 2001, Time named New York mayor Rudy Giuliani the Person of the Year. The following essay on Giuliani is written by Time senior editor and chief political correspondent Eric Pooley.

———□———

Sixteen hours had passed since the Twin Towers crumbled and fell, and people kept telling Rudy Giuliani to get some rest. The indomitable mayor of New York City had spent the day and night holding his town together. He arrived at the World Trade Center just after the second plane hit, watched human beings drop from the sky and—when the south tower imploded— nearly got trapped inside his makeshift command center near the site. Then he led a battered platoon of city officials, reporters and civilians north through the blizzard of ash and smoke, and a detective jimmied open the door to a firehouse so the mayor could revive his government there. Giuliani took to the airwaves to calm and reassure his people, made a few hundred rapid-fire decisions about the security and rescue operations, toured hospitals to comfort the families of the missing and made four more visits to the apocalyptic attack scene.

Now, around 2:30 A.M., Giuliani walked into the Upper East Side apartment of Howard Koeppel and his longtime partner, Mark Hsiao. Koeppel, a friend and supporter of Giuliani's, had been lending the mayor a bedroom suite since June, when Giuliani separated from his second wife, Donna Hanover, and moved out of Gracie Mansion. His suit still covered with ash, Giuliani hugged Koeppel, dropped into a chair and turned on the television—actually watching the full, ghastly spectacle for the first time. He left the TV on through the night in case the terrorists struck again, and he parked his muddy boots next to the bed in case he needed to head out fast. But he was not going to be doing any sleeping. Lying in bed, with the skyscrapers exploding over and over again on his TV screen, he pulled out a book—*Churchill*, the new biography by Roy

Jenkins—turned straight to the chapters on World War II and drank in the Prime Minister's words: I have nothing to offer but blood, toil, tears and sweat.

There is a bright magic at work when one great leader reaches into the past and finds another waiting to guide him. From midmorning on Sept. 11, when Giuliani and fellow New Yorkers were fleeing for their lives, the mayor had been thinking of Churchill. "I was so proud of the people I saw on the street," he says now. "No chaos, but they were frightened and confused, and it seemed to me that they needed to hear from my heart where I thought we were going. I was trying to think, Where can I go for some comparison to this, some lessons about how to handle it? So I started thinking about Churchill, started thinking that we're going to have to rebuild the spirit of the city, and what better example than Churchill and the people of London during the Blitz in 1940, who had to keep up their spirit during this sustained bombing? It was a comforting thought."

With the President out of sight for most of that day, Giuliani became the voice of America. Every time he spoke, millions of people felt a little better. His words were full of grief and iron, inspiring New York to inspire the nation. "Tomorrow New York is going to be here," he said. "And we're going to rebuild, and we're going to be stronger than we were before . . . I want the people of New York to be an example to the rest of the country, and the rest of the world, that terrorism can't stop us."

Sept. 11 was the day that Giuliani was supposed to begin the inevitable slide toward irrelevancy. It was primary-election day in the city, when people would go to the polls to begin choosing his successor. After two terms, his place in history seemed secure: great mayor, not-so-great guy. The first Republican to run the town in a generation, he had restored New York's spirit, cutting crime by two-thirds, moving 691,000 people off the welfare rolls, boosting property values and incomes in neighborhoods rich and poor, redeveloping great swaths of the city. But great swaths of the city were sick of him. People were tired of his Vesuvian temper and constant battles— against his political enemies, against some of his own appointees, against the media and city-funded museums, against black leaders and street vendors and jaywalkers and finally even against his own wife. His marriage to television per- sonality Donna Hanover was a war: ugly headlines, dueling press conferences. Giuliani's girlfriend, a pharmaceutical-sales manager named Judith Nathan, had helped him get through a battle against prostate cancer, and his struggle touched off a wave of concern and appreciation for him. But most New Yorkers seemed ready for Rudy and Judi to leave the stage together and melt into the crowd.

Fate had another idea. When the day of infamy came, Giuliani seized it as if he had been waiting for it all his life, taking on half a dozen critical roles and performing each masterfully. Improvising on the fly, he became America's homeland-security boss, giving calm, informative briefings about the attacks and the extraordinary response. He was the gutsy decision maker, balancing security against symbol- ism, overruling those who wanted to keep the city buttoned up tight, pushing key institutions—from the New York Stock

Exchange to Major League Baseball—to reopen and prove that New Yorkers were getting on with life. He was the crisis manager, bringing together scores of major players from city, state and federal governments for marathon daily meetings that got everyone working together. And he was the consoler in chief, strong enough to let his voice brim with pain, compassion and love. When he said "the number of casualties will be more than any of us can bear," he showed a side of himself most people had never seen.

Giuliani's performance ensures that he will be remembered as the greatest mayor in the city's history, eclipsing even his hero, Fiorello La Guardia, who guided Gotham through the Great Depression. Giuliani's eloquence under fire has made him a global symbol of healing and defiance. World leaders from Vladimir Putin to Nelson Mandela to Tony Blair have come to New York to tour ground zero by his side. French President Jacques Chirac dubbed him "Rudy the Rock." As Jenkins, author of the biography that inspired Giuliani on the night of Sept. 11, told *Time*, "What Giuliani succeeded in doing is what Churchill succeeded in doing in the dreadful summer of 1940: he managed to create an illusion that we were bound to win."

CHAPTER FOUR

SCIENCE, TECHNOLOGY, AND SOCIETY: UNDERSTANDING A NEW KIND OF WARFARE

"Meeting the Challenge"
By Marc Fisher
From **American Journalism Review**
October 2001

Before the September 11 attacks, the American media often walked a fine line between delivering hard news and catering to the public's increasing desire for light entertainment. The hot "news" stories preceding the attacks—a congressman's romantic relationship with a missing intern, a summer of numerous shark attacks, Mariah Carey's nervous breakdown—suddenly seemed even more frivolous and sensationalistic in the wake of such unimaginable tragedy and loss. Throughout the dark day of September 11, however, the American media proved that it had lost none of its journalistic instincts or prowess and still had what it takes to report a truly historic story. In this piece, Marc Fisher, a columnist for the Washington Post *and a regular contributor to the* American Journalism Review, *examines how the attacks were covered by the different news media, including television, radio, newspapers, and the Internet, and assesses their performance.*

———□———

This is why we do what we do.

The video of a jumbo jet slipping into the skyscraper, silently, smoothly, as if this were a normal bit of physics. The photos of human beings, New Yorkers, covered in ash, holding briefcases, wearing work clothes, as if this were how they went to the office that day. The descriptions by reporters who were there: Sonny Kleinfield in the *New York Times*, writing that "on the street there was endless paper and unmatched shoes," and then, on the second day, calling his town "a city of less." Bart Gellman's riveting detail in the *Washington Post*, writing about the man who assembled a fishing rod to try to fetch his car keys from a locked cashier's booth even as fires burned around him: "Civilians did what they could think of, not all of it sensible." John Bussey's harrowing first-person account in the *Wall Street Journal*: "In the silence, as the ash fell like snow, radios crackled: 'Steve, Steve, where are you?'"

We all started the day on television, where the terror ratcheted up in speedy steps, from fluky crash at the World Trade Center, to "Oh, God!" on the network morning shows as the second plane struck, to the ultimate in 24-hour, saturation coverage. We watched Peter Jennings' beard grow, and we were somehow reassured that he did not shave, that through morning, afternoon, evening and on into the night, he did not leave the desk, that he confided in us his uncertainties, that he shared the confusions of each hour. He grew more pale and more vulnerable, as if he knew that we needed him to be human, so that we could be together. We saw Tom Brokaw grow teary, we saw him put on his glasses. We counted on Peter, Tom and Dan to be steady and straight, qualities that

President Bush, in his disturbing darting around the country, failed to communicate.

Up and down the dial, we clicked our clickers, and we saw unrelenting, unbiased, unstinting coverage of unbelievable events. CNN was back in its glory days, its worldwide cast of characters shining through, its conversation for once smart and restrained. Fox News Channel did its image little good; despite cutting edge reporting by Carl Cameron and a vigorous attempt to keep up with the older, bigger guys on the cable block, within hours, Fox's pack of chatterers had slipped into the speculation and name-calling that dominate its daily product.

But it wasn't so much a day to dwell on individual performances as one in which the nation once again collectively turned to the home screen for essential information, for solace, for a sense of direction. It was as if we had returned to the era of three networks; the one story was the media monolith, and we craved the community that comes from a shared viewing experience. TV responded, unselfishly, with precious little grandstanding. But for an over-the-top wallop of saccharine overwriting in a breathless Diane Sawyer narration toward the end of ABC's long first day of coverage, the networks stuck to what was known, told it straight, and stripped away the artifice. It's amazing to see how quickly the music and the fancy graphics and the sparkling animations drop away when there's real news to report.

And then there was radio, once the medium of immediacy, the place we turned to first for a quick info fix before TV could produce its packages, before newspapers could manufacture their industrial product. But radio's ability to serve news has been devastated in these last few years of corporate consolidation, greed and a near-total abdication of responsibility. Result: But for the excellent, comprehensive coverage of National Public Radio and a handful of all-news stations—most notably, wall-to-wall reporting on WTOP in Washington and WCBS and WINS in New York—radio was reduced to simulcasting CNN's TV audio and to delivering maudlin expressions of sorrow by clueless deejays. Could this shameful display spur the industry to get back into the news business? Hardly likely. The triumph of niche formatting and lowest common denominator programming is virtually complete: On the morning after the attack, America's most popular morning man, Howard Stern, was giggling with his sidekicks about genocide.

Luckily, NPR was there, with intelligent pieces and a devotion to giving people time and space to tell their stories. On "All Things Considered," producers let children speak at length about their sense of what the attacks were about. A World Trade Center office worker narrated his own story of escape—riveting radio, words summoning mental images that came closer to the horror than any video could. On "Morning Edition," the tried and true format and Bob Edwards' calming voice created a space where Americans could come together. Even the interstitial music, a trademark of the program, rose to the occasion, as directors selected American elegies— Copland, Ives—sounds that spoke of sorrow, accompanying reports that built understanding: what to tell the children, how Muslim Americans saw the attack, a first-person account of running from the collapsing tower.

The day America joined the rest of the world in daily life with terror and death was also a test for the newest of media, the Internet and its myriad news sites. For the most part, the medium showed that it is simply not ready for prime time. Through no fault of programmers, most news Web sites were just not available throughout the first day, and those that were could not begin to compete with the instant video and nonstop updates of TV.

By the dawn of the day after, however, it was clear that the new-media revolution would be neither televised nor streamed. It was left to the nation's newspapers, to the small-town dailies that called in all hands to pump out extras on Day One, and especially to the couple of dozen big papers that have not succumbed entirely to the cost-cutting frenzy of the past two decades, to show why this business deserves its constitutional protection, and why so many people accept sub-par wages, long hours and public disdain to practice this craft.

From the banner headlines to the gut-wrenching photographs, from stark descriptions to speedily constructed narratives, papers delivered page upon page of stories that brought readers the news, the background, the context. At Pentagon City Mall, the sprawling retail complex a short walk from the still-smoldering Pentagon, I found 47 people in the food court at 10 o'clock in the morning the day after the attack. Thirty-nine of them were sitting at tables with a newspaper spread out in front of them. They were deep into *USA Today*'s dazzling coverage—the perfect selection of pictures, the stories you needed to read, each slug sliced just right. They were well into the third leg of type on David Von Drehle's *Washington Post* essay about what it all meant: "Yesterday's attacks are the dark face of a small world." He ranged from John Brown at Harper's Ferry to Archduke Ferdinand to Leon Trotsky, and he was accessible and fast and caring. He did what only newspapers can do, just as the *Los Angeles Times* did with a front-page reconstruction of "The Choreography of Carnage."

People were buying papers to take home to save, to give to their children and grandchildren. Writers around the country delivered the goods. Jimmy Breslin, writing in *Newsday*, took readers exactly where they would expect him to take them: into the soul of a fireman in lower Manhattan, into the heart of the city of our dreams.

A cop covered with gray collapse dust talks numbly.

"Dead," he says.

"How many do you think?"

He closes his eyes. "God knows."

The first lists speak of 200 dead firefighters and 78 cops. The City of Courage.

Sure, there were excesses. The September 13 edition of *Newsday* carried a piece about the tragic loss of the World Trade Center's 107th floor restaurant, Windows on the World. No, thank you. Not this day.

But such moves were the exception. The news coverage was detailed and deliberate. By Day Two, newspapers were deep into the how and why, comparing U.S. airport security to the far more rigorous efforts of the Israelis and the Swiss, wondering what might have impelled people to jump from the heights of the World Trade Center, baring the efforts of the Palestinian Authority to suppress coverage of street celebrations of America's anguish.

It was only in opinion pieces that emotion took over, the warmongers unleashing their snapping verbs and sizzling adjectives. In the *New York Post*, columnist Steve Dunleavy, whose oeuvre in the *Star* tabloid used to go under the moniker "The Man They Call Mr. Blood and Guts," wrote that the American response "to this unimaginable 21st century Pearl Harbor should be as simple as it is swift . . . kill the bastards . . . A gunshot between the eyes, blow them to smithereens, poison them if you have to . . . As for cities or countries that host these worms, bomb them into basketball courts." Even more refined writers such as Charles Krauthammer and Robert Kagan scrambled to be among the first to advocate outright war.

And of course, the political pundits simply could not help themselves. Forty-eight hours after the towers fell, some smart alecks were already crowning Rudy Giuliani president in '04.

Still, those first hours after the attack were a time to be proud of what we do, to know that despite all the bean counters and all the corporate doublespeak about serving customers, despite the cutbacks and the buyouts, despite the shuttered bureaus and the dumbed-down story lists, there are still editors and reporters and producers and camera people who know that there is a time to drop all our conceits and all our ego trips and to report the hell out of a story and deliver words that matter and pictures that burst with meaning.

"Why Did the World Trade Center Collapse? Science, Engineering, and Speculation"
By Thomas W. Eagar and Christopher Musso
From JOM
2001

Thomas Eagar is the Thomas Lord Professor of Materials Engineering and Engineering Systems at the Massachusetts Institute of Technology. Following the collapse of the World Trade Center, he was one of many scientists, engineers, and architects who sought an explanation of why and how the Twin Towers fell. At the time, numerous theories were circulating. Some believed that the initial impact of the commercial jets had weakened the structural beams of the building to the point that the towers collapsed under their own weight. Others believed that the great amount of fuel contained in the planes' tanks had burned so hot upon impact that the buildings' steel beams had melted into liquid metal. Still more people believed that the trusses—the structures that supported each floor—had been weakened by the intense heat and flames and began to give way, leading to a domino effect of floors crashing down upon floors. Eagar and graduate student Christopher Musso argue for a combination of these factors, all contributing to the massive structural failure of the Twin Towers.

———□———

The collapse of the World Trade Center (WTC) towers on September 11, 2001, was as sudden as it was dramatic; the complete destruction of such massive buildings shocked nearly everyone. Immediately afterward and even today, there is widespread speculation that the buildings were structurally deficient, that the steel columns melted, or that the fire suppression equipment failed to operate. In order to separate the fact from the fiction, we have attempted to quantify various details of the collapse.

The major events include the following:

- The airplane impact with damage to the columns.

- The ensuing fire with loss of steel strength and distortion.

- The collapse, which generally occurred inward without significant tipping.

The Airline Impact

The early news reports noted how well the towers withstood the initial impact of the aircraft; however, when one recognizes that the buildings had more than 1,000 times the mass of the aircraft and had been designed to resist steady wind loads of 30 times the weight of the aircraft, this ability to withstand the initial impact is hardly surprising. Furthermore, since there was no significant wind on September 11, the outer perimeter columns were only stressed before the impact to around 1/3 of their 200 MPa [mean values] design allowable.

The only individual metal component of the aircraft that is comparable in strength to the box perimeter columns of the WTC is the keel beam at the bottom of the aircraft fuselage. While the aircraft impact undoubtedly destroyed several columns in the WTC perimeter wall, the number of columns lost on the initial impact was not large and the loads were shifted to remaining columns in this highly redundant structure. Of equal or even greater significance during this initial impact was the explosion when 90,000 liquid gallons of jet fuel, comprising nearly 1/3 of the aircraft's weight, ignited. The ensuing fire was clearly the principal cause of the collapse.

The Fire

The fire is the most misunderstood part of the WTC collapse. Even today, the media report (and many scientists believe) that the steel melted. It is argued that the jet fuel burns very hot, especially with so much fuel present. This is not true.

Part of the problem is that people (including engineers) often confuse temperature and heat. While they are related, they are not the same. Thermodynamically, the heat contained in a material is related to the temperature through the heat capacity and the density (or mass). Temperature is defined as an intensive property, meaning that it does not vary with the quantity of material, while the heat is an extensive property, which does vary with the amount of material. One way to distinguish the two is to note that if a second log is added to the fireplace, the temperature does not double; it stays roughly the same, but the size of the fire or the length of time the fire burns, or a combination of the two, doubles. Thus, the fact that there were 90,000 liters of jet fuel on a few floors of the WTC does not mean that this was an unusually hot fire. The temperature of the fire at the WTC was not unusual, and it was most definitely not capable of melting steel.

It is known that structural steel begins to soften around 425°C and loses about half of its strength at 650°C. This is why steel is stress relieved in this temperature range. But even a 50% loss of strength is still insufficient, by itself, to explain the WTC collapse. It was noted above that the wind load controlled the design allowables. The WTC, on this low-wind day, was likely not stressed more than a third of the design allowable, which is roughly one-fifth of the yield strength of the steel. Even with its strength halved, the steel could still support two to three times the stresses imposed by a 650°C fire.

The additional problem was distortion of the steel in the fire. The temperature of the fire was not uniform everywhere, and the temperature on the outside of the box columns was clearly lower than on the side facing the fire. The temperature along the 18 meter long joists was certainly not uniform. Given the thermal expansion of steel, a 150°C temperature difference from one location to another will produce yield-level residual stresses. This produced distortions in the slender structural steel, which resulted in buckling failures. Thus, the failure of the steel was due to two factors: loss of strength due to the temperature of the fire, and loss of structural integrity due to distortion of the steel from the non-uniform temperatures in the fire.

The Collapse

Nearly every large building has a redundant design that allows for loss of one primary structural member, such as a column. However, when multiple members fail, the shifting loads eventually overstress the adjacent members and the collapse occurs like a row of dominoes falling down.

The perimeter tube design of the WTC was highly redundant. It survived the loss of several exterior columns due to aircraft impact, but the ensuing fire led to other steel failures. Many structural engineers believe that the weak points—the limiting factors on design allowables—were the angle clips that held the floor joists between the columns on the perimeter wall and the core structure. With a 700 Pa floor design allowable, each floor should have been able to support approximately 1,300 tons beyond its own weight. The total weight of each tower was about 500,000 tons.

As the joists on one or two of the most heavily burned floors gave way and the outer box columns began to bow outward, the floors above them also fell. The floor below (with its 1,300 ton design capacity) could not support the roughly 45,000 tons of ten floors (or more) above crashing down on these angle clips. This started the domino effect that caused the buildings to collapse within ten seconds, hitting bottom with an estimated speed of 200 kilometers per hour. If it had been free fall, with no restraint, the collapse would have only taken eight seconds and would have impacted at 300 km/hr. It has been suggested that it was fortunate that the WTC did not tip over onto other buildings surrounding the area. There are several points that should be made. First, the building is not solid; it is 95 percent air and, hence, can implode onto itself. Second, there is no lateral load, even the impact of a speeding aircraft, which is sufficient to move the center of gravity one hundred feet to the side such that it is not within the base footprint of the structure. Third, given the near free-fall collapse, there was insufficient time for portions to attain significant lateral velocity. To summarize all of these points, a 500,000 ton structure has too much inertia to fall in any direction other than nearly straight down.

Was the WTC Defectively Designed?

The World Trade Center was not defectively designed. No designer of the WTC anticipated, nor should have anticipated, a 90,000 liter Molotov cocktail on one of the building floors. Skyscrapers are designed to support themselves for three hours in a fire even if the sprinkler system fails to operate. This time should be long enough to evacuate the occupants. The WTC towers lasted for one to two hours—less than the design life, but only because the fire fuel load was so large. No normal office fires would fill 4,000 square meters of floor space in the seconds in which the WTC fire developed. Usually, the fire would take up to an hour to spread so uniformly across the width and breadth of the building. This was a very large and rapidly progressing fire (very high heat but not unusually high temperature). Further information about the design of the WTC can be found on the World Wide Web.

Where Do We Go from Here?

The clean-up of the World Trade Center will take many months. After all, 1,000,000 tons of rubble will require 20,000 to 30,000 truckloads to haul away the material. The asbestos fire insulation makes the task hazardous for those working nearby. Interestingly, the approximately 300,000 tons of steel is fully recyclable and represents only one day's production of the U.S. steel industry. Separation of the stone and concrete is a common matter for modern steel shredders. The land-filling of 700,000 tons of concrete and stone rubble is more problematic. However, the volume is equivalent to six football fields, 6–9 meters deep, so it is manageable.

There will undoubtedly be a number of changes in the building codes as a result of the WTC catastrophe. For example, emergency communication systems need to be upgraded to speed up the notice for evacuation and the safest paths of egress. Emergency illumination systems, separate from the normal building lighting, are already on the drawing boards as a result of lessons learned from the WTC bombing in 1993. There will certainly be better fire protection of structural members. Protection from smoke inhalation, energy-absorbing materials, and redundant means of egress will all be considered.

A basic engineering assessment of the design of the World Trade Center dispels many of the myths about its collapse. First, the perimeter tube design of the towers protected them from failing upon impact. The outer columns were engineered to stiffen the towers in heavy wind, and they protected the inner core, which held the gravity load. Removal of some of the outer columns alone could not bring the building down. Furthermore, because of the stiffness of the perimeter design, it was impossible for the aircraft impact to topple the building.

However, the building was not able to withstand the intense heat of the jet fuel fire. While it was impossible for the fuel-rich, diffuse-flame fire to burn at a temperature high enough to melt the steel, its quick ignition and intense heat caused the steel to lose at least half its strength and to deform, causing buckling or crippling. This weakening and deformation caused a few floors to fall, while the weight of the stories above them crushed the floors below, initiating a domino collapse.

It would be impractical to design buildings to withstand the fuel load induced by a burning commercial airliner. Instead of saving the building, engineers and officials should focus on saving the lives of those inside by designing better safety and evacuation systems.

As scientists and engineers, we must not succumb to speculative thinking when a tragedy such as this occurs. Quantitative reasoning can help sort fact from fiction, and can help us learn from this unfortunate disaster. As Lord Kelvin said,

"I often say . . . that when you can measure what you are speaking about, and express it in numbers, you know something about it; but when you cannot measure it, when you cannot express it in numbers, your knowledge is of a meager and unsatisfactory kind; it may be the beginning of knowledge, but you have scarcely, in your thoughts, advanced to the stage of science, whatever the matter may be."

We will move forward from the WTC tragedy and we will engineer better and safer buildings in the future based, in part, on the lessons learned at the WTC. The reason the WTC collapse stirs our emotions so deeply is because it was an intentional attack on innocent people. It is easier to accept natural or unintentional tragedies; it is the intentional loss of life that makes us fear that some people have lost their humanity.

"Cultural Schizophrenia"
By Malise Ruthven
From Opendemocracy.net
September 27, 2001

"Why do they hate us?" This was a question that was asked throughout the United States on September 11, 2001, and after. What would drive Islamic militants to sacrifice their own lives while committing murder against thousands of innocent people, all in the name of God? Was Islam itself to blame? Was it the fault of an imperialistic Western foreign policy? What caused this? Much has been written in an attempt to find plausible answers to these questions. Malise Ruthven, an author and Islamic studies scholar, tackles these questions in her essay, "Cultural Schizophrenia." Ruthven argues that much of the violence and anger of Islamic extremists arises from a culture clash between the modern Western world and traditional Islamic society. Threatened by the encroachment of technology, popular Western culture, and an increasingly secular global society, many Muslims (who are often poor and politically powerless in their own countries) lash out and try to attack the West with the very Western technology that they despise—hijacked airplanes, explosives, nuclear material, chemical weapons, and even the media.

—□—

In the immediate aftermath of the skybombing of the World Trade Centre in New York, and the Pentagon in Washington, anyone with a minimum of human sympathy will be overwhelmed by feelings of rage and despair. Politicians, responding to the public mood, declare "war on terrorism." The airline industry goes into the proverbial nosedive. The stock markets tumble and experts predict that to the cost in human sorrow will be added the pain of economic recession. Muslim statesmen and spokesmen, fearful of the consequences of America's ire, denounce the attack as contrary to everything that Islam stands for. But Palestinian Muslims are shown on TV dancing in the streets, and in Pakistan Islamic militants are shown demanding jihad or "holy war" against the United States in the event of an attack on Afghanistan.

Pakistan, pressured by the United States, agrees to join the "Coalition against Terrorism" despite fears that collaboration with the U.S. will meet resistance from the Taliban and their Pakistani supporters. Yet a U.S. attack on Afghanistan could trigger the overthrow of the moderate, pro-Western government headed by General (now President) Pervez Musharraf, placing Islamist fingers on the nuclear button long before President George W. Bush's National Missile Defense initiative is ready for action. An American attack on Afghanistan could well precipitate the overthrow of pro-Western regimes not only in Pakistan, but in Saudi Arabia and the Gulf, Egypt, Jordan and North Africa. Should this occur the attack on New York and Washington will no longer be seen as acts of "nihilistic" violence as some commentators maintain. Seen from the terrorists' perspective it was an act of provocation aimed at unleashing a global conflict between a revitalised "Islam" and "The West."

Whether or not George Bush's "War Against Terrorism" will generate such direful consequences remains to be seen. The dust has to settle and the debris cleared, with its hideous burden of human remains, before the international ramifications become fully apparent. Yet certain patterns are already beginning to emerge.

Contrary to the rhetoric of politicians, the attack was far from being "cowardly" or "mindless." A brilliantly executed feat of planning, co-ordination and execution backed by an astonishing degree of courage, the attack exemplifies something that has come to characterize the modern (or "post-modern") world: the union of the symbolic with the actual, the mythical with the material, in a single act of destruction shown live on television.

Solidarities of Tribe and Faith

Using the language of a Texan sheriff the U.S. President has announced Osama bin Laden is "wanted dead or alive" for mass murder in New York City and Washington. The evidence linking the Saudi dissident with the atrocity appears to be largely circumstantial and it is doubtful if, on present reckoning, it would stand up in a court of law.

One should, of course, be cautious before drawing firm conclusions. But if press reports fed by leaks from the FBI are accurate, the finger points directly to Osama bin Laden. Although the networks over which he presides are loosely structured—he does not apparently use his own satellite phone in case the calls are traced to him—the fact that the hijackers are thought to be Saudis and Yemenis from the same region as his own family suggests that the inner circle of al-Qa'ida, its Praetorian guard, may have been directly involved.

There are precedents. Throughout Islamic history rebels and reformers—or, to be more precise, rebels against the established order who present themselves as "renovators" (mujaddids)—have allied themselves with closely-knit tribal communities (often their own) with a view to achieve power and purge the state of corruption. The fourteenth-century philosopher and historian Ibn Khaldun (d. 1406) who lived in Spain and North Africa before moving to Egypt, used the word 'asabiya (group-feeling or solidarity) to describe the tight human bonds that held these movements together. In Ibn Khaldun's historical theory, the 'asabiya of groups moving from the periphery to the centre under the banner of reformed or revitalised Islam was the motor of historic and dynastic change. The 'asabiya of the group that planned and executed the hijackings, which may have involved hundreds of individuals in different countries communicating via coded e-mails and mobile phones, appears to have been formidable: not only was nothing leaked, but some people with foreknowledge of the attack appear to have made fortunes in airline stocks, possibly for use in future operations.

Many hundreds of Muslims may be numbered among the victims of the attack on the World Trade Center. In their "War against America" the terrorists do not distinguish between their co-religionists and others. Most Westerners find it paradoxical that people who have demonstrated a remarkable degree of technical proficiency in their operations—training as pilots, co-ordinating a highly complex logistical operation involving the co-ordination of airline schedules with carefully worked-out dummy runs—should hold "fanatical" or "fundamentalist" religious views. Newspaper accounts focus on the rewards of martyrdom promised for those "who die in the path of Allah," which include the ministrations of 72 virgins in Paradise. The political passions that motivate terrorists in other traditions (such as Irish republicanism) are not usually linked so directly to a belief in the carnal pleasures of immortality. Yet no successful movement of this kind, whether religious, political or a combination of both, has ever lacked for martyrs willing to kill and be killed for the "cause."

Modernising the War on Unbelief

There is, however, a substantial body of research which indicates that fundamentalist movements in the Abrahamic traditions (Christianity, Judaism and Islam) are particularly attractive to graduates in the applied sciences (such as engineering, computer programming and other highly technical trades). Graduates in the arts and humanities who are trained to read texts critically may be less susceptible to the simplistic religious messages put forward by such movements. Technical specialisations discourage critical thinking. It may be that technicians from "pre-Enlightenment" cultures operate on separate epistemological tracks. The cultural, emotional and spiritual knowledge embedded in the religious tradition they inherit has not been integrated with the technical knowledge they acquire by training and by rote . . .

The Saudi Boomerang

It may be too early to say how far the men who hijacked the four American airliners and committed the greatest terrorist atrocity in history were influenced by Qutbist doctrines. Osama bin Laden is reported to have studied with Sayyid Qutb's brother Muhammad after his "conversion" to Islam. Muhammad initially shared his brother's radicalism, although in the debate among the militants that followed Sadat's assassination, Muhammad eventually sided with the moderates who rejected the strategy of pronouncing takfir (declaration of infidelity) against other Muslims. But if press reports are to be believed, at least one of the hijackers, the Egyptian-born Muhammad Ata, fits the Qutbist mould in many respects. A brilliant student of architecture and town-planning at the technical university of Hamburg (in Germany), he seems to have experienced a dramatic conversion to Islamic fundamentalism shortly before completing his thesis (the equivalent of an MSc in town planning) which earned him a 1.0—the highest possible mark. After returning from Egypt where he had temporarily grown a thick bushy beard he began shying from any physical contact with women—the hallmark of fundamentalist piety. Thereafter he appears to have led a double life, showing unusual courtesy and consideration to strangers while planning and training for his murderous attack . . .

The cultural and religious schizophrenia experienced by a man like Muhammad Ata is microcosmic when compared to that of a whole society. Modern Saudi Arabia where Osama bin Laden's father, a street-porter from Aden, made a fortune by constructing palaces for princes, exemplifies the paradox of a high-tech society wedded to a pre-modern conservative theology. The chief religious dignitary, Sheikh bin Baz, still holds a Ptolemaic or geocentric view of the cosmos based on his reading of the Quran. Yet Saudi Arabia has bought into the U.S. space programme, sending the first and so far the only Muslim astronaut into orbit.

Oil, the source of Saudi wealth, has been the "fuel of fundamentalism"—ever since the Stewart brothers of Southern California used the money they made in the oil business to fund the conservative Christian publications that brought the "F-word" into the English language. Because the extraction process is largely technical and depersonalised, the creation of oil wealth (unlike wealth acquired through manufacturing) has not necessitated the intellectual or social transformations and the evolving relations of production that occurred in older industrialised societies.

Saudi Arabia buys in its technology wholesale and houses its guest-workers and hired technocrats in foreigners-only compounds in order to protect its society and the Wahhabi version of Islam underpinning it from foreign influences. This strategy, however, has failed to insulate it against the radical religio-political currents sweeping through the region. Paradoxically, it has assisted their spread through its sponsorship of such organisations as the Muslim Brotherhood and the Muslim World League. Having assisted in the globalisation of radical Islam Saudi Arabia is now one of its principal targets. What happened in New York and Washington exemplifies the contradictions between Saudi Arabia's hired technocracy and its religious conservatism.

"At War with Liberty"
By Stephen J. Schulhofer
From **The American Prospect**
March 1, 2003

When American soil is threatened, civil liberties are often the first victim of the government's rush to provide greater security and protection to the nation and its institutions. In this essay, Stephen J. Schulhofer, the Robert B. McKay Professor of Law at New York University, discusses the ramifications of the USA PATRIOT Act, which was written and approved by Congress in the immediate aftermath of the attacks. It was designed to help the Justice Department fight terrorism by granting law enforcement new and expanded powers to monitor the private lives of individuals through search warrants, electronic surveillance, and wiretapping, for example. The bill was passed nearly unanimously by Congress, even though it contained some disturbing measures, such as the requirement that, if asked, bookstores and libraries disclose what titles have been bought or borrowed by certain individuals. At the time of the USA PATRIOT Act's signing into law, homeland security was considered the government's highest priority, and many Americans were willing to sacrifice some privacy in order to create a more secure nation. With the passage of time, however, the act's possible infringements on cherished constitutional rights seem to many Americans to pose a grave threat to democracy. Since the

time of this article's publication, Jose Padilla, the so-called
"dirty bomber" mentioned in this piece, continues to be detained
in the Navy brig in South Carolina. It was not until March 1,
2003, that he was finally allowed to meet with his lawyer.

———□———

As expected, September 11 has prompted an expansion of
law-enforcement powers at almost every level. And who would
have it otherwise? For those of us who live and work in
Manhattan, 9-11 was not a single horrific day but an extended
nightmare. For weeks, kiosks, store windows and parks displayed fliers by the thousands, pleading for information about
loved ones still missing. National Guard units seemed to be
everywhere. Day after day, the air—gray and acrid—carried
the smell of burning flesh.

No, the "war" metaphor is not just convenient political
spin. And despite shameless hyping of "sleeper cells" and color-
coded threat levels, no responsible person can dismiss the
danger of devastating future attacks. Actions to strengthen law
enforcement are not simply the product of panic or paranoia.

But the particulars are troubling, and worse. Predictably,
there has been overreaction and political grandstanding. More
surprising is the neglect. The administration has inexcusably
swept aside urgent security needs while it continues to win
public acclaim for toughness by targeting and scapegoating
civil liberties.

An accounting of the state of our liberties should begin
with the positives. To his credit, the president has preached
tolerance and respect for our Muslim neighbors. Unlike previ-
ous wartime governments, his administration has not sought

to prosecute dissenters for political speech, has not attempted anything comparable to the internment of Japanese Americans during World War II and (technically, at least) has not tried to suspend the writ of habeas corpus.

But to measure performance by these standards is to set the bar terribly low; these were sorry historical embarrassments. And 9-11 has already produced several comparable missteps. The administration's efforts to stymie habeas corpus rival the civil-liberties low points of prior wars, as does Bush's determination (wholly without precedent) to hold American citizens indefinitely on disputed charges without affording them a trial in any forum, civil or military. Also without precedent are the oddly imbalanced means chosen to fight this battle. Never before in American history has an administration stinted on many homeland- and national-security expenditures and made tax cuts its top priority at a time of war. Conventional wisdom about striking a balance between liberty and security obscures the fact that responses to 9-11 are deeply flawed from both perspectives.

Surveillance and Privacy

The USA PATRIOT Act, passed in October 2001, expanded government surveillance powers in multiple directions. Investigators won new authority to track Internet use and to obtain previously confidential business and educational records. Prosecutors gained access to the broad search and wiretap powers of the Foreign Intelligence Surveillance Act. The Department of the Treasury expanded its authority to require banks, brokers and other businesses to report cash transactions and "suspicious activities," which include any transaction that differs from ones the customer typically conducts. Though the Department of Justice created a furor with its proposal to encourage voluntary snooping by private citizens, the Treasury Department regulations require private citizens and businesses to become eyes and ears for the government.

Many Americans are ready to sacrifice these sorts of privacies to obtain any nugget of information about al-Qaeda plans. Nonetheless, the rollback of privacy rights has three flaws that should trouble us all. First, worries about terrorism provide no reason to expand law-enforcement power across the board. Yet FBI and Treasury Department agents can use most of their new powers to investigate allegations of prostitution, gambling, insider trading or any other offense. There is no excuse for exploiting 9-11 to intrude on privacy in pursuit of these unrelated goals.

Second, accountability measures, though neglected in the rush to pass the PATRIOT Act, need not impair the usefulness of the new powers but, if well designed, would actually enhance them. The FBI's "Carnivore" system for spying on e-mail, for example, desperately needs procedures to preserve audit trails and ensure the accountability of agents who have access to it.

Finally, additional information is useless unless our agencies are able to make sense of it. It's now well known that before 9-11, the FBI and the CIA had important clues about the plot in hand, but as one FBI agent put it, "We didn't know what we knew." Because a large part of what we lack is not raw data but the ability to separate significant intelligence from "noise," pulling more information into government files may aggravate rather than solve the problem. Even before 9-11, Treasury Department officials complained that the staggering volume of reports they received—more than a million every month—was interfering with enforcement. Absent a substantial infusion of resources (which the administration has failed to provide), powerful new surveillance tools can give us only a false sense of comfort.

Unleashing the FBI

Last May headlines featured for days the startling news that in July and August 2001, agents in Minneapolis and Phoenix, Ariz., had urged investigations of Zacarias Moussaoui and the flight schools, only to be stifled by FBI headquarters—an enormous blunder. In response, Attorney General John Ashcroft called a press conference to denounce "bureaucratic restrictions" that were preventing FBI agents from doing their jobs.

The rules he had in mind grew out of extensive FBI abuses in the 1950s and 1960s. Free to pursue random tips and their own hunches, agents back then intimidated dissidents, damaged reputations and produced thousands of dossiers on public figures, private citizens, political parties and social movements. By 1975, FBI headquarters held more than half a million domestic intelligence files.

Such sprawling dragnets are as inefficient as they are abusive. Rules to rein them in were adopted in 1976 by President Gerald Ford and have been reaffirmed by every president since. Nonetheless, Ashcroft ridiculed these guidelines as absurdly restrictive. He said—incorrectly—that the rules barred FBI agents from surfing the Internet and even from observing activities in public places. He announced that he was solving this problem by allowing FBI agents to operate with much less supervision.

The civil-liberties community responded with outrage. But far from hurting Ashcroft's popularity, the criticism reinforced his intended message: that defendants' rights had hobbled law enforcement. The failure to pursue the flight-school leads was in effect blamed on the American Civil Liberties Union, and the Justice Department presented itself as taking firm, corrective action.

What actually occurred was rather different. One set of guidelines the attorney general relaxed governs investigations of "general crimes"—gambling, theft and other offenses not related to terrorism. The other guidelines he loosened govern investigations of domestic terrorist groups. Unnoticed in the brouhaha, the rules governing international terrorism cases— the ones that apply to al-Qaeda—weren't affected by the changes at all.

Behind the screen of this public-relations maneuver, damage was inflicted in several directions. Public frustration with central oversight was understandable under the circumstances, but none of the guidelines, even the more restrictive domestic regimes, impeded the kinds of investigative steps the Minneapolis and Phoenix agents had urged. What the field offices needed was better supervision, not less of it. Yet Ashcroft's actions obscured responsibility for FBI missteps, and instead of censure, the FBI was

rewarded with greater discretion. As in the case of the
PATRIOT Act, fear of terrorism offered an occasion for bait
and switch: The guideline revisions don't in any way
address the al-Qaeda threat that preoccupies the public, yet
they leave us with heightened risks to civil liberties and
much less effective management at the FBI.

Detentions and Secrecy

In the months following 9-11, federal agents arrested approximately 1,200 foreign nationals. Hundreds—the precise number
is unknown—were held for months before being cleared and
released; others remain in detention, ostensibly awaiting
deportation. Courts are still sorting through the many issues
the detentions pose.

Particularly troubling is the extraordinary secrecy surrounding these sweeps. The government has refused to release
the names of any of the detainees. Individuals charged and
afforded immigration hearings find those hearings closed to the
press and even to their own families.

The government's justifications for secrecy are revealing.
Secrecy, Ashcroft stated, is necessary to protect the privacy
of detainees. Because many of them desperately wanted
their names made public—so that aid organizations and
lawyers could contact them—and because the Justice
Department could have afforded secrecy to detainees who
requested it, the privacy claim was painfully disingenuous. In
litigation, Justice Department lawyers added the argument
that releasing the names of terrorists would give the terrorists'
cohorts clues about the progress of the investigation. This

"roadmap" argument, though not entirely frivolous, is embarrassingly thin. Because all detainees have the right to make phone calls, and because gag orders have not been imposed on their lawyers and family, detainees who really are terrorists can easily signal their confederates.

Secrecy across the board, without any obligation to present case-specific reasons for it in court, has less to do with the war on terrorism than with the administration's consistent efforts, firmly in place before 9-11, to insulate executive action from public scrutiny. The cumulative effect of these efforts is an unprecedented degree of power—an attempt simultaneously to cut off the right to counsel or judicial review and any ability of the press to report what happens to individuals arrested on U.S. soil.

The Assault on Habeas Corpus

Jose Padilla, the so-called dirty bomber who allegedly planned to explode a bomb laced with radioactive material, was arrested in May 2002 at Chicago's O'Hare Airport and held for a month as a material witness. Counsel was appointed for him, and he was due to be brought to court on June 11. Instead, two nights before that date, President Bush decided that Padilla was an "enemy combatant," a finding that the Justice Department tenaciously argues cannot be reviewed by any federal judge.

That night, without notice to his court-appointed counsel, Padilla was taken from federal detention in Manhattan, put on a military plane bound for South Carolina and thrown into a Navy brig. That was June 9, and Padilla hasn't been heard from since. The government has refused to let him speak to the press or to his own attorney, and has done everything in its power to deny him access to the courts.

Enemy infiltrators have posed acute threats to public safety before, notably during the Civil War. Lincoln, a straightforward man, responded by suspending the writ of habeas corpus.

That is not the Bush administration style. When Padilla's lawyer, Donna Newman, tried to file a habeas petition on her client's behalf, the government suggested no need to suspend the writ. Its argument was the "narrow" one that the Padilla petition was invalid because he hadn't signed it. Having deliberately blocked all contact between Padilla and the outside world, the government told the court that a valid habeas petition required his signature, that Newman couldn't sign for him (how do we know that Padilla still wanted her to obtain his release?) and that his own lawyer had no standing to ask the court's help because she had no "significant relationship" with him. Federal Judge Michael Mukasey ultimately dismissed these arguments as frivolous. He ruled that Newman had to be granted access to her client and that he would review the "enemy combatant" designation to be sure it was supported by "some evidence."

Mukasey's decision was announced on Dec. 9, yet Padilla remains incommunicado. As of early February, the government was continuing to find new reasons why Newman should be denied all contact with him, though Judge Mukasey, losing patience, probably will insist that a visit be permitted soon. After eight months (and counting), Padilla will eventually get to see his lawyer, and the judge will decide whether "some evidence" supports the detention . . .

The government says its approach is rooted in its need to continue incommunicado interrogation, for an indefinite period, in order to find out what Padilla knows. If he hasn't talked at this point, after eight months of interrogation, it's hard to believe another eight or 10 months will do the trick, or that whatever Padilla knows isn't stale. But we can't rule out the possibility that after many months (or years) of isolation, a suspect might eventually reveal something useful.

The problem with that argument is the Constitution—not just its fine points but the very idea of a government under law. If the mere possibility of a useful interrogation is enough to support indefinite detention incommunicado, no rights and no checks and balances are available at all, except when the executive chooses to grant them. If a ruler in any other country claimed unilateral powers of this sort, Americans would be quick to recognize the affront to the most basic of human rights . . .

The American homeland has been threatened before. The Civil War brought four years of fighting on American soil, and Hawaii was a theater of active military operations throughout World War II. In both situations, the military argued the need for displacing civilian courts, and in both situations, the Supreme Court rejected the argument explicitly. "Martial law," the Court said in Ex Parte Milligan, "cannot arise from a threatened invasion. The necessity must be actual and present . . . such as effectually closes the courts . . . If martial law is continued after the courts are reinstated, it is a gross usurpation of power."

The presumption against military detention, whenever civilian courts are functioning, is not merely a doctrinal technicality. The central premise of government under law is that executive officials, no matter how well intentioned, cannot be allowed unreviewable power to imprison a citizen. Even in times of dire emergency, the Supreme Court has been consistent and emphatic on this point.

The White House does not exaggerate when it talks about the dangers of al-Qaeda and the need for a "war" on terrorism. Precisely because the risks of a terrorist attack are so serious, administration policies should be troubling to every American. The decision to blame civil liberties and to draw attention away from other aspects of an effective counterterrorism strategy is a dangerous choice.

CHAPTER FIVE

GLOBAL CONNECTIONS: THE UNITED STATES AND THE WORLD BEYOND

A Reading Delivered by British Prime Minister Tony Blair at an Interfaith Memorial Service for British Victims of the Attack on the World Trade Center
St. Thomas Church, New York
September 21, 2001

Great Britain has been a close friend of the United States since the beginning of the twentieth century. Often, it has found its politics more in line with those of its former rebellious colony than with those of its neighbors in Europe. British prime minister Tony Blair immediately stepped forward as one of the first international leaders to offer assistance with the September 11 recovery effort as well as with the war on terror declared by Bush several days later. Britain shared the burden of the post–September 11 world partly because it shared the pain of that day. It lost more citizens in the World Trade Center attacks—sixty-seven—than any country other than the United States. At a memorial service for these British victims at St. Thomas Church in midtown Manhattan ten days after the attacks, Blair delivered a eulogy whose words successfully conveyed the pain and confusion that many people felt at the time but were not yet able to express.

—◻—

There is no reading, there are no words, that can truly comfort those who are grieving the loss of their loved ones today; and no matter how we try to make sense of it all it is hard, so hard, to do.

Nine days on, there is still the shock and disbelief; there is anger; there is fear; but there is also, throughout the world, a profound sense of solidarity; there is courage; there is a surging of the human spirit.

We wanted to be here today, to offer our support and sympathy to the families of the lost ones. Many are British. Amid the enormity of what has happened to America, nobody will forget that this was the worst terrorist attack on British citizens in my country's history.

The bonds between our countries for so long so strong, are even stronger now. For my reading I have chosen the final words of *The Bridge of San Luis Rey* written by Thornton Wilder in 1927. It is about a tragedy that took place in Peru, when a bridge collapsed over a gorge and five people died.

"A witness to the deaths, wanting to make sense of them and explain the ways of God to his fellow human beings, examined the lives of the people who died, and these words were said by someone who knew the victims, and who had been through the many emotions, and the many stages, of bereavement and loss.

"But soon we will die, and all memories of those five will have left earth, and we ourselves shall be loved for a while and forgotten. But the love will have been enough; all those impulses of love return to the love that made them. Even memory is not necessary for love. There is a land of the living and a land of the dead, and the bridge is love. The only survival, the only meaning."

Statement by Pakistani Prime Minister Pervez Musharraf
September 12, 2001

In the hours and days following the September 11 attacks, the outpouring of sympathy from the international community was enormous and largely unanimous in its expression of sorrow, outrage, and solidarity. Old allies and longtime enemies joined together to condemn the suicide attacks and offer assistance and prayers to the American people. Pakistan, a nation with a large Muslim majority, has long had a difficult relationship with the United States, which has favored its enemy and neighbor India. Yet, the day after the attacks, the prime minister of Pakistan, Pervez Musharraf, released a strongly worded statement addressed to his own people in which he harshly condemned the attacks and all forms of terrorism and urged Pakistanis living in the United States to take part in relief efforts. Pakistan went on to become a key ally in President George W. Bush's war on terror. Given the militancy of a large number of Pakistan's Muslims, Musharraf's offers of support and friendship to the United States required great political courage.

My dear Pakistanis!

The despicable and devastating act against innocent people in New York and Washington has caused great anguish and concern among the Government and the people of Pakistan. As a peace-loving nation we join the world community in strongly condemning these brutal acts and the consequent loss of precious lives. Terrorism is a threat to humanity and to the human civilization. Pakistan condemns all acts of terrorism anywhere in the world and shares the sorrow and grief of the people of the United States.

I urge upon all of you, living in the United States of America, to extend all possible help and assistance to all victims.

I urge you to step forward and donate much needed blood for the injured. Step out and provide your service and your resources to all those who need them there.

I am confident you would rise to the occasion and assist, help and assuage the grieved. My heart goes out to the families of all those who have suffered and particularly to the families of those who lost their lives whether Americans, Pakistanis or from any other country.

Address by U.S. President George W. Bush to a Special Joint Session of Congress
Washington, D.C.
September 20, 2001

The speech President George W. Bush delivered to a special joint session of Congress on September 20, 2001, was one of the more important speeches he gave in the aftermath of the attacks and perhaps of his entire presidency. In this speech, Bush outlined his first concrete plans for a response to the terror attacks, calling upon the radical Islamic Afghani government of the time—the Taliban—to turn over Osama bin Laden and end all terrorist training, planning, and support operations within the country. If these demands were not met, war would follow, in Afghanistan and in any country that harbored terrorists. Bush had declared an all-out war on terror. Within weeks, the United States had invaded Afghanistan and overthrown the Taliban. Iraq was next on Bush's list, and an invasion began in early 2003, partly to prevent Iraqi dictator Saddam Hussein's use of weapons of mass destruction (WMD) he had allegedly stockpiled. At this point, no WMD have been located, and after he was found in December 2003, Hussein claimed that he never had any WMD. Osama bin Laden, however, is still at large. Meanwhile, the war on terror threatens to spread to Iran and Southeast Asia, further widening an already diffuse and free-ranging conflict.

———□———

Americans have many questions tonight. Americans are asking: Who attacked our country? The evidence we have gathered all points to a collection of loosely affiliated terrorist organizations known as al Qaeda. They are the same murderers indicted for bombing American embassies in Tanzania and Kenya, and responsible for bombing the USS *Cole.*

Al Qaeda is to terror what the mafia is to crime. But its goal is not making money; its goal is remaking the world—and imposing its radical beliefs on people everywhere.

The terrorists practice a fringe form of Islamic extremism that has been rejected by Muslim scholars and the vast majority of Muslim clerics—a fringe movement that perverts the peaceful teachings of Islam. The terrorists' directive commands them to kill Christians and Jews, to kill all Americans, and make no distinction among military and civilians, including women and children.

This group and its leader—a person named Osama bin Laden—are linked to many other organizations in different countries, including the Egyptian Islamic Jihad and the Islamic Movement of Uzbekistan. There are thousands of these terrorists in more than 60 countries. They are recruited from their own nations and neighborhoods and brought to camps in places like Afghanistan, where they are trained in the tactics of terror. They are sent back to their homes or sent to hide in countries around the world to plot evil and destruction.

The leadership of al Qaeda has great influence in Afghanistan and supports the Taliban regime in controlling most of that country. In Afghanistan, we see al Qaeda's vision for the world.

Afghanistan's people have been brutalized—many are starving and many have fled. Women are not allowed to attend school. You can be jailed for owning a television. Religion can be practiced only as their leaders dictate. A man can be jailed in Afghanistan if his beard is not long enough.

The United States respects the people of Afghanistan— after all, we are currently its largest source of humanitarian aid—but we condemn the Taliban regime. It is not only repressing its own people, it is threatening people everywhere by sponsoring and sheltering and supplying terrorists. By aiding and abetting murder, the Taliban regime is committing murder.

And tonight, the United States of America makes the following demands on the Taliban: Deliver to United States authorities all the leaders of al Qaeda who hide in your land. Release all foreign nationals, including American citizens, you have unjustly imprisoned. Protect foreign journalists, diplomats and aid workers in your country. Close immediately and permanently every terrorist training camp in Afghanistan, and hand over every terrorist, and every person in their support structure, to appropriate authorities. Give the United States full access to terrorist training camps, so we can make sure they are no longer operating.

These demands are not open to negotiation or discussion. The Taliban must act, and act immediately. They will hand over the terrorists, or they will share in their fate.

I also want to speak tonight directly to Muslims throughout the world. We respect your faith. It's practiced freely by many millions of Americans, and by millions more in countries that America counts as friends. Its teachings are good and peaceful, and those who commit evil in the name of Allah blaspheme the name of Allah. The terrorists are traitors to their own faith, trying, in effect, to hijack Islam itself. The enemy of America is not our many Muslim friends: it is not our many Arab friends. Our enemy is a radical network of terrorists, and every government that supports them.

Our war on terror begins with al Qaeda, but it does not end there. It will not end until every terrorist group of global reach has been found, stopped and defeated . . . Americans should not expect one battle, but a lengthy campaign, unlike any other we have ever seen. It may include dramatic strikes, visible on TV, and covert operations, secret even in success. We will starve terrorists of funding, turn them one against another, drive them from place to place, until there is no refuge or no rest. And we will pursue nations that provide aid or safe haven to terrorism. Every nation, in every region, now has a decision to make. Either you are with us, or you are with the terrorists. From this day forward, any nation that continues to harbor or support terrorism will be regarded by the United States as a hostile regime. . .

This is not, however, just America's fight. And what is at stake is not just America's freedom. This is the world's fight. This is civilization's fight. This is the fight of all who believe in progress and pluralism, tolerance and freedom.

We ask every nation to join us. We will ask, and we will need, the help of police forces, intelligence services, and banking systems around the world. The United States is grateful that many nations and many international organizations have already responded—with sympathy and with support. Nations from Latin America, to Asia, to Africa, to Europe, to the Islamic world. Perhaps the NATO Charter reflects best the attitude of the world: An attack on one is an attack on all.

The civilized world is rallying to America's side. They understand that if this terror goes unpunished, their own cities, their own citizens may be next. Terror, unanswered, can not only bring down buildings, it can threaten the stability of legitimate governments. And you know what—we're not going to allow it . . .

"Blaming America First"
By Todd Gitlin
From **Mother Jones**
January/February 2002

In the days after September 11, 2001, many people felt an unprecedented sense of unity and common cause with their fellow Americans, as old political divisions and philosophical disagreements seemed less important in the wake of such tragedy and threat. But debate and divisiveness had not disappeared. While many conservatives called for an aggressive military response to the terrorist attacks, some Leftist thinkers attempted to make sense of what happened by examining the injustice of a great deal of American foreign policy, especially in the Middle East, where the suffering and violence Americans experienced on September 11 is an almost daily reality. What right do Americans have to grieve, they asked, when their government has caused so much sorrow to so many people around the world? Todd Gitlin is an author and professor of journalism and sociology at Columbia University in New York. During the 1960s, he was active in leading student protest movements against the Vietnam War and served as president of Students for a Democratic Society (SDS). In this piece, he argues that American sorrow is as just as any other nation's sorrow. So, too, is the nation's desire to strike back when struck.

———□———

As shock and solidarity overflowed on September 11, it seemed for a moment that political differences had melted in the inferno of Lower Manhattan. Plain human sympathy abounded amid a common sense of grief and emergency. Soon enough, however, old reflexes and tones cropped up here and there on the left, both abroad and at home—smugness, acrimony, even schadenfreude [taking pleasure in someone else's distress], accompanied by the notion that the attacks were, well, not a just dessert, exactly, but . . . damnable yet understandable payback . . . rooted in America's own crimes of commission and omission . . . reaping what empire had sown. After all, was not America essentially the oil-greedy, Islamdisrespecting oppressor of Iraq, Sudan, Palestine? Were not the ghosts of the Shah's Iran, of Vietnam, and of the Cold War Afghan jihad rattling their bones? Intermittently grandiose talk from Washington about a righteous "crusade" against "evil" helped inflame the rhetoric of critics who feared—legitimately—that a deepening war in Afghanistan would pile human catastrophe upon human catastrophe. And soon, without pausing to consider why the vast majority of Americans might feel bellicose as well as sorrowful, some on the left were dismissing the idea that the United States had any legitimate recourse to the use of force in self-defense—or indeed any legitimate claim to the status of victim.

I am not speaking of the ardent, and often expressed, hope that September 11's crimes against humanity might eventually elicit from America a greater respect for the whole of assaulted humanity. A reasoned, vigorous examination of U.S. policies, including collusion in the Israeli occupation, sanctions against Iraq, and support of corrupt regimes in Saudi Arabia and Egypt, is badly needed. So is critical scrutiny of the administration's actions in Afghanistan and American unilateralism on many fronts. But in the wake of September 11 there erupted something more primal and reflexive than criticism: a kind of left-wing fundamentalism, a negative faith in America the ugly.

In this cartoon view of the world, there is nothing worse than American power—not the woman-enslaving Taliban, not an unrepentant Al Qaeda committed to killing civilians as they please—and America is nothing but a self-seeking bully. It does not face genuine dilemmas. It never has legitimate reason to do what it does. When its rulers' views command popularity, this can only be because the entire population has been brainwashed, or rendered moronic, or shares in its leaders' monstrous values.

Of the perils of American ignorance, of our fantasy life of pure and unappreciated goodness, much can be said. The failures of intelligence that made September 11 possible include not only security oversights, but a vast combination of stupefaction and arrogance—not least the all-or-nothing thinking that armed the Islamic jihad in Afghanistan in order to fight our own jihad against Soviet Communism—and a willful ignorance that not so long ago permitted half the citizens of a flabby, self-satisfied democracy to vote for a man unembarrassed by his lack of acquaintanceship with the world.

But myopia in the name of the weak is no more defensible than myopia in the name of the strong. Like jingoists who consider any effort to understand terrorists immoral, on the grounds that to understand is to endorse, these hard-liners disdain complexity. They see no American motives except oil-soaked power lust, but look on the bright side of societies that cultivate fundamentalist ignorance. They point out that the actions of various mass murderers (the Khmer Rouge, bin Laden) must be "contextualized," yet refuse to consider any context or reason for the actions of Americans.

If we are to understand Islamic fundamentalism, must we not also trouble ourselves to understand America, this freedom-loving, brutal, tolerant, shortsighted, selfish, generous, trigger-happy, dumb, glorious, fat-headed powerhouse?

Not a bad place to start might be the patriotic fervor that arose after the attacks. What's offensive about affirming that you belong to a people, that your fate is bound up with theirs? Should it be surprising that suffering close-up is felt more urgently, more deeply, than suffering at a distance? After disaster comes a desire to reassemble the shards of a broken community, withstand the loss, strike back at the enemy. The attack stirs, in other words, patriotism—love of one's people, pride in their endurance, and a desire to keep them from being hurt anymore. And then, too, the wound is inverted, transformed into a badge of honor. It is translated into protest ("We didn't deserve this") and indignation ("They can't do this to us"). Pride can fuel the quest for justice, the rage for punishment, or the pleasures of smugness. The dangers are obvious. But it should not be hard to understand that the American flag sprouted in the days after September 11, for many of us, as a badge of belonging, not a call to shed innocent blood.

This sequence is not a peculiarity of American arrogance, ignorance, and power. It is simply and ordinarily human. It operates as clearly, as humanly, among nonviolent Palestinians attacked by West Bank and Gaza settlers and their Israeli soldier-protectors as among Israelis suicide-bombed at a nightclub or a pizza joint. No government anywhere has the right to neglect the safety of its own citizens—not least against an enemy that swears it will strike again. Yet some who instantly, and rightly, understand that Palestinians may burn to avenge their compatriots killed by American weapons assume that Americans have only interests (at least the elites do) and gullibilities (which are the best the masses are capable of).

In this purist insistence on reducing America and Americans to a wicked stereotype, we encounter a soft anti-Americanism that, whatever takes place in the world, wheels automatically to blame America first. This is not the hard anti-Americanism of bin Laden, the terrorist logic under which, because the United States maintains military bases in the land of the prophet, innocents must be slaughtered and their own temples crushed. Totalitarians like bin Laden treat issues as fodder for the apocalyptic imagination. They want power and call it God. Were Saddam Hussein or the Palestinians to win all their demands, bin Laden would move on, in his next video, to his next issue.

Soft anti-Americans, by contrast, sincerely want U.S. policies to change—though by their lights, such turnabouts are well-nigh unimaginable—but they commit the grave moral error of viewing the mass murderer (if not the mass murder) as nothing more than an outgrowth of U.S. policy. They not only note but gloat that the United States built up Islamic fundamentalism in Afghanistan as a counterfoil to the Russians. In this thinking, Al Qaeda is an effect, not a cause; a symptom, not a disease. The initiative, the power to cause, is always American.

But here moral reasoning runs off the rails. Who can hold a symptom accountable? To the left-wing fundamentalist, the only interesting or important brutality is at least indirectly the United States' doing. Thus, sanctions against Iraq are denounced, but the cynical mass murderer Saddam Hussein, who permits his people to die, remains an afterthought. Were America to vanish, so, presumably, would the miseries of Iraq and Egypt.

In the United States, adherents of this kind of reflexive anti-Americanism are a minority (isolated, usually, on campuses and in coastal cities, in circles where reality checks are scarce), but they are vocal and quick to action. Observing flags flying everywhere, they feel embattled and draw on their embattlement for moral credit, thus roping themselves into tight little circles of the pure and the saved.

The United States represents a frozen imperialism that values only unbridled power in the service of untrammeled capital. It is congenitally, genocidally, irremediably racist. Why complicate matters by facing up to America's self-contradictions, its on-again, off-again interest in extending rights, its clumsy egalitarianism coupled with ignorant arrogance? America is seen as all of a piece, and it is hated because it is hateful—period. One may quarrel with the means used to bring it low, but low is only what it deserves.

So even as the smoke was still rising from the ground of Lower Manhattan, condemnations of mass murder made way in some quarters for a retreat to the old formula and the declaration that the "real question" was America's victims—as if there were not room in the heart for more than one set of victims.

And the seductions of closure were irresistible even to those dedicated, in other circumstances, to intellectual glasnost. Noam Chomsky bent facts to claim that Bill Clinton's misguided attack on a Sudanese pharmaceutical plant in 1998 was worse by far than the massacres of September 11. Edward Said, the exiled Palestinian author and critic, wrote of "a superpower almost constantly at war, or in some sort of conflict, all over the Islamic domains." As if the United States always picked the fight; as if U.S. support of the Oslo peace process, whatever its limitations, could be simply brushed aside; as if defending Muslims in Bosnia and Kosovo—however dreadful some of the consequences—were the equivalent of practicing gunboat diplomacy in Latin America or dropping megatons of bombs on Vietnam and Cambodia.

From the Indian novelist Arundhati Roy, who has admirably criticized her country's policies on nuclear weapons and development, came the queenly declaration that "American people ought to know that it is not them but their government's policies that are so hated." (One reason why Americans were not exactly clear about the difference is that the murderers of September 11 did not trouble themselves with such nice distinctions.) When Roy described bin Laden as "the American president's dark doppelganger" and claimed that "the twins are blurring into one another and gradually becoming interchangeable," she was in the grip of a prejudice invulnerable to moral distinctions.

Insofar as we who criticize U.S. policy seriously want Americans to wake up to the world—to overcome what essayist Anne Taylor Fleming has called our serial innocence, ever renewed, ever absurd—we must speak to, not at, Americans, in recognition of our common perplexity and vulnerability. We must abstain from the fairy-tale pleasures of oversimplification. We must propose what is practical—the stakes are too great for the luxury of any fundamentalism. We must not content ourselves with seeing what Washington says and rejecting that. We must forgo the luxury of assuming that we are not obligated to imagine ourselves in the seats of power.

Generals, it's said, are always planning to fight the last war. But they're not alone in suffering from sentimentality, blindness, and mental laziness disguised as resolve. The one-eyed left helps no one when it mires itself in its own mirror-image myths. Breaking habits is desperately hard, but those who evade the difficulties in their purist positions and refuse to face all the mess and danger of reality only guarantee their bitter inconsequence.

TIMELINE

September 11, 2001 8:46 am — Hijacked American Airlines Flight 11 out of Boston, Massachusetts, crashes into the nort tower of the World Trade Center (WTC).

9:03 am — A second hijacked jet, United Airlines Flight 175, also from Boston, crashes into the south tower of the WTC. Both towers are now burnin

9:17 am — The Federal Aviation Administration (FAA) shuts down all New York City area airports.

9:21 am — The Port Authority of New York and New Jersey closes all bridges and tunnels into and out of the New York area. The FAA halts all air traffic in the United States, the first time in its history it has done so.

9:38 am — American Airlines Flight 77 from Washington, D.C., crashes into the Pentagon, which is immediately evacuated.

9:45 am — The White House is evacuated.

10:05 am — The south tower of the WTC collapses.

10:10 am — A fourth hijacked plane, United Airlines Fligh 93 from Newark, New Jersey, crashes in Shanksville, Pennsylvania, southeast of Pittsburgh. It was possibly headed for the White House, Capitol Building, or Camp Davi

10:28 am — The north tower of the WTC collapses.

10:45 am — All federal office buildings in Washington, D.C., are evacuated.

11:02 am —— Manhattan south of Canal Street is evacuated.

1:27 pm —— A state of emergency is declared in Washington, D.C.

6:54 pm —— President George W. Bush returns to Washington, D.C., after spending much of the day zigzagging across the country in Air Force One.

October 7, 2001 —— The United States begins bombing Afghanistan, whose radical Islamist government, the Taliban, is thought to be sheltering and supporting Osama bin Laden and other Al Qaeda operatives.

October 19, 2001 —— U.S. Special Forces begin ground attacks in Afghanistan.

October 26, 2001 —— The USA PATRIOT Act—a domestic anti-terrorist bill that grants law enforcement new search and seizure powers—is signed into law.

May 30, 2002 —— Eight months and nineteen days after the collapse of the WTC, the recovery effort at Ground Zero comes to an official end. Thanks to 3.1 million hours of labor provided by Ground Zero workers, 1.8 million tons (or 108,342 truckloads) of debris were removed from the site.

November 25, 2002 —— The cabinet-level Department of Homeland Security is created, replacing an earlier and less powerful Office of Homeland Security formed in late September 2001.

March 1, 2003 —— The alleged mastermind of the September 11 attacks, Khalid Shaikh Mohammed, is arrested in Pakistan.

FOR MORE INFORMATION

Web Sites

Due to the changing nature of Internet links, the Rosen Publishing Group, Inc., has developed an online list of Web sites related to the subject of this book. This site is updated regularly. Please use this link to access the list:

http://www.rosenlinks.com/canf/niel

FOR FURTHER READING

Benjamin, Daniel, and Steven Simon. *The Age of Sacred Terror: Radical Islam's War Against America*. New York: Random House, 2002.

Bergen, Peter L. *Holy War, Inc.: Inside the Secret World of Osama bin Laden*. New York: Free Press, 2002.

Bernstein, Richard, et al. *Out of the Blue: A Narrative of September 11, 2001*. New York: Times Books, 2002.

Fink, Mitchell, and Lois Mathias. *Never Forget: An Oral History of September 11, 2001*. New York: Regan Books, 2002.

Glanz, James, and Eric Lipton. *City in the Sky: The Rise and Fall of the World Trade Center*. New York: Times Books, 2003.

Kirtzman, Andrew. *Rudy Giuliani: Emperor of the City*. New York: HarperCollins, 2001.

Levitas, Mitchel, et al. *A Nation Challenged: A Visual History of 9/11 and Its Aftermath*. New York: Times Books, 2002.

Life magazine. *One Nation: America Remembers September 11, 2001*. New York: Little, Brown & Co., 2001.

Magnum Photographers. *New York September 11*. New York: PowerHouse Books, 2001.

Miller, John, and Michael Stone, with Chris Mitchell. *The Cell: Inside the 9/11 Plot and Why the FBI and CIA Failed to Stop It*. New York: Hyperion, 2003.

New York Times. Portrait: 9/11/01: The Collected "Portraits of Grief" from the New York Times. New York: Times Books, 2002.

Posner, Gerald L. *Why America Slept: The Failure to Prevent 9/11*. New York: Random House, 2003.

Wormser, Richard. *American Islam: Growing Up Muslim in America*. New York: Walker & Co., 1994.

ANNOTATED BIBLIOGRAPHY

Bernstein, Richard, et al. "Threats and Responses: Pieces of a Puzzle; On Plotters' Path to U.S., a Stop at bin Laden Camp." *New York Times*, September 10, 2002, section A. Copyright © 2002 by The New York Times Co. Reprinted with permission.

Richard Bernstein reconstructs the long planning process that went into Al Qaeda's September 11 attacks, from the initial inspiration and selection of the hijackers to flight training and final preparations on the night of September 10.

Blair, Tony. Address at an interfaith memorial service. New York, September 21, 2001.

This is the text of a reading given by British prime minister Tony Blair at a memorial service for the sixty-seven British victims of the World Trade Center attacks held at St. Thomas Church in midtown Manhattan ten days after the tragedy.

Bush, George W. Address to a special joint session of Congress, Washington, D.C., September 20, 2001.

This is an excerpt from President George W. Bush's address to a joint session of Congress in which he remembers the victims of the recent September 11 attacks and outlines his administration's proposed response to the attacks—the so-called war on terror.

Corbin, Jane. *Al-Qaeda: In Search of the Terror Network That Threatens the World*. New York: Thunder's Mouth Press, 2003.

Jane Corbin is an award-winning senior correspondent for the British Broadcasting Corporation (BBC). In order to shed light on the shadowy terrorist network, Corbin conducted hundreds of interviews with key eyewitnesses, investigators, and intelligence officers around the world.

Dwyer, Jim, et al. *Two Seconds Under the World: Terror Comes to America—The Conspiracy Behind the World Trade Center Bombing.* New York: Crown Publishers, Inc., 1994.

Copyright ©1994 by Jim Dwyer and David Kocieniewski, Deidre Murphy, Peg Tyre. Used by permission of Crown Publishers, a division of Random House, Inc.

The authors, reporters who covered the story for *New York Newsday*, use interviews with confidential sources, NYPD reports, and trial testimony to develop the story of the first World Trade Center bombing in 1993.

Eagar, Thomas W., and Christopher Musso. "Why Did the World Trade Center Collapse? Science, Engineering, and Speculation." *JOM*, Vol. 53, No. 12 (2001): 8–11.

Reprinted with permission from: Eagar, Thomas W., and Christopher Musso. "Why Did the World Trade Center Collapse? Science, Engineering, and Speculation" *JOM*, 53 (12), pp. 8–11, copyright © 2001 by TMS (The Minerals, Metals, and Materials Society), Warrendale, PA.

In this article from *JOM* (the member journal of the Minerals, Metals, and Materials Society), Thomas Eagar, an engineering professor at the Massachusetts Institute of Technology, and graduate student Christopher Musso seek to explain exactly how and why the towers of the World Trade Center collapsed following the crashing of two hijacked commercial planes into their sides on September 11, 2001.

Fisher, Marc. "Meeting the Challenge." *American Journalism Review*, October 2001. Reprinted by permission of *American Journalism Review*.

Marc Fisher, a columnist for the *Washington Post* and a regular contributor to the *American Journalism Review*, examines how the September 11 attacks were covered by the different news media, including television, radio, newspapers, and the Internet, and assesses their performances.

Gitlin, Todd. "Blaming America First." *Mother Jones*, January/February 2002. Copyright © 2002, Foundation for National Progress.

Todd Gitlin, an author, professor of journalism and sociology at Columbia University in New York, and liberal activist, vigorously disagrees with some of his fellow liberals who claim that, because of the past and present crimes perpetrated by American foreign policy, the United States has no right of self-defense, legitimate claim to victim status, or freedom to feel grief in the wake of the September 11 attacks.

Gopnik, Adam. "The City and the Pillars." *New Yorker*, September 24, 2001. Copyright © 2002 Adam Gopnik. Reprinted by permission from *The New Yorker*.

Adam Gopnik, an author and art and culture critic for *The New Yorker*, wistfully describes New York's final seconds of blissful naïveté before the first hijacked plane struck the north tower of the World Trade Center on September 11, 2001, as well as the surreal and nightmarish aftermath.

Halberstam, David. *Firehouse*. New York: Hyperion, 2002. Copyright © 2002. Reprinted by permission of David Halberstam.

Pulitzer Prize–winning author David Halberstam tells the tragic story of his local New York firehouse during the day of September 11, 2001. Of the thirteen men from Engine 40, Ladder 35, who responded to the call that morning, only one came back to the firehouse alive. In piecing together what happened to these thirteen firefighters, Halberstam also describes the inner workings of a firehouse, its traditions, routines, and complex social structure.

Langewiesche, William. *American Ground: Unbuilding the World Trade Center*. New York: North Point Press, 2003.
This book is based on a series of articles William Langewiesche wrote for the *Atlantic Monthly*. Given unrestricted access to Ground Zero during the World Trade Center salvage operation, the author is able to tell the entire story of "the Pile," from the moment of the towers' destruction to the departure of the last truckload of rubble from the ruins a little less than nine months later.

Longman, Jere. *Among the Heroes: United Flight 93 and the Passengers and Crew Who Fought Back*. New York: Harper-Collins Publishers, 2002. Epilogue & excerpt from chapter 11 (totaling 2000 words). Copyright © 2002 by Jere Longman. Reprinted with permission of HarperCollins Publishers Inc.
In order to piece together the chain of events on United Flight 93—the jet that crashed in Shanksville, Pennsylvania—*New York Times* reporter Jere Longman conducted hundreds of interviews with family members of the passengers and reviewed the dozens of cell phone calls made to and from the passengers during the final terrifying and frantic moments of their ordeal.

Musharraf, Pervez. Statement by the Pakistani prime minister to his people. September 12, 2001.

This is the text of a statement released by Pakistani prime minister Pervez Musharraf to Pakistanis at home and abroad, expressing the nation's sorrow over the September 11 attacks and its condemnation of all terrorist acts.

Plotz, David. "The Pentagon's Strangely Festive Ceremony." Slate.com. September 11, 2002. Retrieved August 2003 (http://slate.msn.com/id/2070796/). Copyright © 2002. First published in Slate Magazine, www. Slate.com. Reprinted with permission. Slate is a trademark of Microsoft Corporation.

David Plotz, a journalist based in Washington, D.C., covered the attack on the Pentagon, as well as the ceremony held there on the first anniversary of September 11. In this piece, Plotz tries to understand and explain why the Pentagon victims have received so little attention compared to the other victims of September 11.

Pooley, Eric. "Mayor of the World." *Time*, December 31, 2001. Copyright © 2001 Time Inc. Reprinted by permission.

In 2001, three months after the September 11 terrorist attacks, *Time* named New York mayor Rudy Giuliani its Person of the Year. This essay on Giuliani is written by *Time* senior editor and chief political correspondent Eric Pooley.

Ruthven, Malise. "Cultural Schizophrenia." Opendemocracy.net. September 27, 2001. Retrieved August 2003 (http://www.opendemocracy.net/debates/article-5-44-103.jsp).

In this essay, Malise Ruthven, an author and Islamic studies scholar, argues that much of the violence and anger of

Islamic extremists arises from a culture clash between the
modern Western world and traditional Islamic society.

Schulhofer, Stephen J. "At War with Liberty." *The American
Prospect*, Vol. 14, No. 3, March 1, 2003.
    In this essay, Stephen J. Schulhofer, a New York University
    law professor, discusses the possible threat posed to civil lib-
    erties and personal privacy by the 2001 USA PATRIOT Act.

Singer, Mark. "Home Is Here." *The New Yorker*, October
15, 2001.
    Mark Singer, a staff writer for *The New Yorker*, traveled to
    Dearborn, Michigan—the second-largest Arab enclave in
    the world outside the Middle East—to find out how the
    Arab American community felt about the September 11
    attacks and how they have been treated by their neighbors
    since that day.

White, E. B. *Here Is New York*. New York: Little Bookroom, 1999.
    Written in the summer of 1948 after a move to Maine, E.
    B. White looks back and offers a warm and loving tribute
    to the glittering, dynamic, and vulnerable city that
    launched his writing career and captivated his imagination.

Yardley, Jim, et al. 2001. "A Nation Challenged: The
Mastermind; A Portrait of the Terrorist: From Shy Child to
Single-Minded Killer." *The New York Times*, October 10,
2001, section B, p. 9. Copyright © 2001 by The New York
Times Co. Reprinted with permission.
    Yardley seeks to understand how Mohamed Atta, a shy,
    serious, well-off, and well-loved young man, could
    embrace religious extremism, violence, and murder and
    go about it in such a cool and calculating way.

INDEX

About the Editor

Fletcher Haulley graduated from New York University in 2003 with a degree in history. He is also the author of *The Department of Homeland Security*.

Cover © AFP/Getty Images, Inc.

Designer: Tom Forget; Series Editor: John Kemmerer